# Table of Contents

Further Resources for the Intersection of Faith and Psychology

References

# Sinful Selves or Sacred Souls

## Personality Typologies in Biblical Discourse

by

**Dr. ant**

endorses the information the organization or website may provide or recommendations it may make.

Please remember that Internet websites listed in this work may have changed or disappeared between when this work was written and when it is read.

Sinful Selves or Sacred Souls: Personality Typologies in Biblical Discourse

**Contents**

**Introduction**

In the elucidation of the human condition, both faith and psychology present themselves as critical yet seemingly disparate lenses through which to examine the enigmatic tapestry of the mind, soul, and behaviors that define our existence. This introductory exposition endeavors to construct a bridge between these two spheres of understanding, elucidating the manner in which the revealed truth can converge with the structure of our cerebral landscapes to provide a compelling, comprehensive view of personhood.

Throughout history, the quest to fathom the depths of the self has yielded a myriad of typologies, characterizations that seek to classify and explain the variances in human disposition and action. It is here, within the realms of typologies, that an intricate web connecting the psychological and the spiritual emerges, paving the road for a substantial dialogue between theologies of human nature and the rigors of scientific inquiry.

The psyche, a paradoxical constellation of elements both seen and unseen, stands as the frontier for this exploration. It offers fertile ground for understanding how biblical tenets of human nature and sin interplay with dispositions and inclinations manifested in behavior and thought patterns. Thus, the importance of typologies extends far beyond the mere categorization of traits; instead, it opens a conduit to a profounder grasp of our nature and guides us in realizing our full potential in the light of divine grace.

To delineate the essence of the self, inclusive of the fissures and fragments birthed by sin, entails a recognition of the inherent complexity of our being. This complexity can be discerned through the variegated lenses that typologies provide. Yet, such frameworks do not stand alone; they are intersected and enlivened by a biblical world perspective that posits humanity as fashioned in the divine image, possessing an innate dignity and an ordained purpose.

The current discourse materializes from two wellsprings of wisdom: the empirical and the eternal. The cerebrum, with its tapestry of neural networks and functional complexities, has been charted meticulously by science, even as the soul's silent whispers echo through the corridors of faith. A biblical tapestry of anthropology serves as a crucial touchstone in comprehending the intersection of such cerebral formation with the character of the individual; a plethora of typologies carving out the features of personality.

Historically, myriad models have arisen to capture the essence of personality—each a mirror reflecting a particular facet of the human experience. From the classical balance of Hippocrates' four humors to the modern clarity of the Myers-Briggs Type Indicator, these typologies stand as testaments to the inexhaustible diversity of human demeanor. Hence, it is within this confluence of ideas that we examine the nuances that define individuality and collectively comprise the mosaic of humanity.

In scrutinizing typologies through a biblical lens, certain patterns demand our attention—the delicate balance of Martha and Mary within Type A and Type B personalities, the relational imperatives of FIRO-B directly paralleling scriptural precepts, or the four humors finding consonance with the temperaments conveyed within the sacred texts. Each of these frameworks holds the potential to unlock deeper understandings of self and divinity when cast against the light of Scripture.

Moreover, in the sieve of these typologies, one may sift the grains of Jungian archetypes alongside biblical figures, unearthing an alignment that transcends their temporal planes. The probing mind is thus ushered through the doorway of epistemology towards a haven of synergetic clarity. This harmony encapsulates the transcendent aim of this pursuit: to reconcile the observations of the psyche with the profound truth revealed through faith.

The knowledge that stems from this unification is not merely academic. Instead, it beckons us toward practical reflections and applications. How do the steadfast qualities of biblical personas mirror modern assessments such as the DISC Profile? In what ways do ancient sinful propensities align with the pitfalls of contemporary personality diagonetics? These are the questions to which our inquiry aspires to respond, mapping the confluence of vice and virtue against the timeless backdrop of Scripture.

Significantly, this study does not seek to replace the insights of psychiatry or to deride the rigor of academia, but rather to enhance these with a perspective that views humanity through the lens of divine revelation. This is an offering—a synthesis of tradition, faith, and scientific pursuit designed to be accessible to the theologian and the psychiatrist, the pastor, and the professor alike.

As we traverse this path, it is incumbent upon us to maintain a spirit of humility and openness, recognizing that the integration of these vast fields of knowledge is a process that must be undergirded by both grace and reason, each informing and refining the other. Thus, the end goal is not simply the defense of a biblical worldview but the fostering of a more profound, well-rounded understanding of the human psyche in the light of that worldview.

This introduction has set forth the stage ready for the unfolding tableau that wends through the various realms of typology and theology. A journey that beckons the reader to move beyond mere classification to a place where the amalgamation of individuality and unity, pathology and sanctity, comes into full view. Here, we seek nothing less than a holistic vision, a place where psychological insight meets theological depth at the crossroads of sanctification and personal growth. It is a vision that asserts that each soul, each mind, breathes with a purpose ordained by virtue of its creation and its Creator.

**Setting the Scene: The Convergence of Faith and Psychology**

In the melodious orchestra of human inquiry, faith and
psychology stand as juxtaposed strings, each resounding with its
own timbre yet harmonizing in the search for understanding the
human condition. The terrain where these disciplines meet is
rich and, for some, unexpectedly congruent. It's in the tapestry
of the mind and the soul that the convergence of faith and
psychology is not only possible but is, indeed, manifestly fruitful.

The psychological realm has long grappled with the nature of
the self, the essence of personality, and the underpinnings of
human behavior. We probe the essence of cognition, emotion,
and behavior with ever-deepening acuity. Yet, these
investigations often unfold devoid of spiritual or theological
reference points. Conversely, the terrain of faith—particularly
within the Christian tradition—proffers a lens through which to
view the human person as not merely a confluence of biological
processes but endowed with a soul, created in a divine image,
and engaged in an existential pilgrimage towards
transcendental truth (Sillberzahn et al., 2018).

The insightful traveler, venturing into the annals of human
experience, finds that the psychological canon offers insights
that echo cardinal truths discernible in theological
anthropology. For the Roman Catholic, the University Professor,

and the Psychiatrist alike, the inquiry into human nature navigates between the cerebral and the spiritual, the quantifiable and the mysterious. The totality of the person encompasses these spheres, for the biological, the psychological, and the spiritual dimensions are inherently interwoven in the fabric of our being (Coe & Hall, 2010).

The synthesis of faith and psychology demands an appreciation for the empirical rigor of scientific inquiry alongside the conviction that human beings carry within them a divine spark. It is within this synthesis that we wrestle with foundational questions about the very nature of selfhood. We discern shadows of spiritual truths within the workings of the mind and echoes of psychological insights within Scriptural revelation.

What then can psychology bring to the table in this dialogue with faith? Equipped with robust methodologies, assessments, and typologies, psychology can illuminate the consistencies, varieties, and idiosyncrasies of personality. It can offer insight into human behavior and motivation—into the 'whys' that lurk beneath the 'whats' of our actions.

Yet, these insights, if left isolated from the domain of the spirit, are incomplete. Just as the body without the spirit is lifeless, so too is a conception of personality that neglects the soul's yearning for the transcendent, for communion with the Creator, for the redemptive narrative that faith traditions hold dear (Entwistle, 2015).

In defense of a biblical worldview and the understanding of human nature intrinsic to it, one is tasked with interpreting the organization of the brain and the mosaic of personality through the unsullied lens of Revealed Truth. The Scriptures and sacred tradition convey a vision of personhood in which psychological complexities are not merely anomalies to be dissected but are entwined with the cosmic struggle of sin, grace, and redemption.

In this convergence, the sacramental imagination of the Christian tradition can coalesce with the discerning eye of psychology to offer a comprehensive anthropology. Where psychology delineates the contours of the psyche, faith narrates the story of the psyche's redemption. Together, faith and psychology can attend to the needs of the whole person, addressing maladies of both mind and soul with a dual repertoire of therapy and theology.

As the quest for understanding leads us into ever deeper explorations of the human person, one cannot eschew the insights of either domain. There is profound wisdom in the psychological understanding of human nature that aligns, in many respects, with the nature of humanity as depicted in Biblical texts—texts that serve as an atlas for countless on their spiritual journeys. The ways in which personality typologies, such as those explored by Friedman, Jung, or Keirsey, can be studied through a biblical lens, accords with our endeavor to bridge these realms, to seek out harmony and synthesis.

The convergence of faith and psychology is not simply an academic exercise but a sacred duty. For within it lies the potential to fortify our intellectual appreciation for the beauty and dignity of the human person, to deepen our understanding of the self, and to inspire a more profound pastoral care that addresses both the mind and the heart. This convergence grants us a language that articulates the complexities of our humanity and a toolkit that equips us to minister to others in their totality.

It must be acknowledged, however, that this joint venture is not void of challenges. The path towards integration is marked by potential pitfalls and paradoxes. The empirical demands of science and the mysteries of faith require a thoughtful navigation that honors the integrity of both. To advance, then, one must exhibit a measured vigilance, ensuring that neither discipline is misappropriated nor diminished in service to the other.

For those who dare to embrace this convergence, the undertaking is no less than a vocation—an invitation to discern and serve the complex tapestry of human existence. Therein, an inquisitive empathy is fostered, igniting a desire to perceive the face of the divine in the spectrum of human experience. It is an endeavor that engages the fullest exercise of reason, the deepest stirrings of the heart, and the most earnest supplications of the soul.

In traversing the terrain where faith and psychology meet, we find neither contradiction nor competition, but rather a call to contemplate the human person in a more expansive and profound light. This convergence is an immeasurable gift, one that offers the promise of an enlightened comprehension and a more compassionate response to the human condition. As such, it is essential that we continue to nurture this dialogue in the service of truth, healing, and holistic well-being.

The presence of this intersection within this text is not incidental but intentional, for it is essential to any substantive discourse on the nature of the self, seen through the prism of both sacred doctrine and psychological science. Let us embark upon this journey with both the analytical mind of the scholar and the contemplative spirit of the believer, that we might fully embrace the convergence of faith and psychology in our quest to understand and serve the human person.

**The Importance of Typologies in Understanding the Self**

The pursuit of self-awareness can be likened to a sojourn through a labyrinth where each turn reveals a deeper sense of our identity and purpose. Within the framework of this scholarly endeavor, typologies emerge as compelling tools that facilitate our comprehension of the multifaceted nature of the human persona. Therefore, the importance of typologies in understanding the self warrants a contemplative exploration, particularly as it intersects with a biblical worldview and the tenets of Christian anthropology.

At their core, typologies serve to categorize and simplify the complexities inherent in human behavior and personality. The church, much like the field of psychiatry, acknowledges that each individual embodies unique traits and tendencies that contribute to their distinctiveness (Cole, 2015). Far from the reductionist approach, typologies provide a language through which we may articulate the variegated tapestry of human experience.

In the endeavor to meld these categorizations with the teachings of faith, one must recognize that typologies do not exist in isolation from the divine narrative. Rather, they are man's attempt to systematize the imago Dei, the reflection of God's image in each human spirit (Macek, 1996). This emanation confers upon us the ability to discern and subsequently align our behaviors with the virtues espoused in sacred scripture.

One must consider that the embrace of typologies does not entail capitulation to a secular understanding of the self. Instead, when evaluated in the light of the Divine Revelation, typologies assume a transformative capacity, guiding individuals towards an amplified understanding of their God-given temperament. The ultimate aim of this illumination is to foster a harmonious relationship with the Creator, self, and the wider community (Tan, 2009).

The typological framework helps to illustrate the variegated human responses to divine grace and sin. As we categorize, we must be cautious not to confine the wondrous creation God has made to mere boxes, but rather to appreciate the depth and breadth of diversity within the unity of the human family. Typologies provide a grid for grasping the nuance within that unity and for appreciating the manifold ways God's grace operates within diverse temperaments (Tan, 2009).

Moreover, the application of typologies within a faith context encourages introspection and a quest for personal growth that is anchored in Christian virtue. Personality types become a platform for understanding our inclinations towards certain sins or proclivities, hence stirring within us a call to conversion and the cultivation of the fruits of the spirit (Galatians 5:22-23).

Considering these aspects, it becomes evident that typologies can vastly enrich our spiritual maturity. As we learn of different personality frameworks, we can better discern our strengths and weaknesses, and how we may serve the body of Christ with our unique gifts (1 Corinthians 12:12-27). It is an introspective path that encourages us to aspire to the likeness of Christ within the context of our intrinsic design (Tan, 2009).

When integrating typologies into the Christian framework, one must exercise prudence, ensuring that these categorizations do not stand in opposition to the sanctity of the individual. Each type, while useful for understanding, must not dictate or limit a person's capacity for divine grace and personal transformation. The goal is to employ these types as guides rather than deterministic molds (James, 2015).

It is also pivotal that when we engage with typologies, we remain mindful of their origins and limitations. While these systems can be insightful, they are ultimately human constructs and must be subordinate to the truths claimed by faith. Typologies should be viewed as pathways to enhance our Christian walk rather than replace or eclipse the profound mystery of the human experience as revealed by God.

The confluence of typologies with the journey of faith leads us to a more profound communion with God, as we discern our propensities in light of the divine plan for sanctification. This sanctification process is deeply personal and yet universally applicable, manifesting uniquely within each personality type as it is refined by the truths of the Gospel (Jones, 2010).

Furthermore, within the Catholic tradition, there's an acknowledgment that the true understanding of self can't be fully realized apart from an understanding of community. Typologies, therefore, equip us to navigate interpersonal relationships within the ecclesial body, allowing us to communicate and minister effectively across diverse personalities (Tan, 2009).

The spiritual life is not static but dynamic, and the application of typologies becomes a pivotal aspect in the cultivation of a responsive and evolving spiritual disposition. This analytical approach to understanding the self, tempered by the grace of God, ushers in a life lived intentionally in the pursuit of holiness.

In the synthesis of typologies with Christian anthropology, the ultimate objective remains the glorification of God through the sanctification of self. By these means, we traverse beyond mere self-awareness into self-transcendence, where understanding our typological makeup becomes instrumental in fulfilling our God-ordained destinies (Hempel & Bartkowski, 2008).

In conclusion, the importance placed on typologies within the context of understanding the self reflects a resolute conviction in their utility for spiritual growth and self-knowledge. These schemas are not an end but a vehicle through which individuals can chart a course towards greater conformity to the image of Christ. In this pursuit, they serve as valuable instruments harmonized with Revealed Truth, guiding the sojourners of faith toward a deeper realization of their identity and purpose in God's overarching narrative.

## Chapter 1: Biblical Worldview of Humanity and Sin

In the intricate dance between the sacred text and human comprehension, our quest finds its compass in a biblical worldview. This chapter navigates the deep waters of humanity's nature, reflecting on the potent combination of grace and fallenness that characterizes our existence. This pilgrimage through the annals of sin and sanctification begins, aptly, with the theological bedrock upon which our understanding stands: human nature as depicted in Holy Scripture.

The sacred writ posits a profound and complex perspective on human beings. Crafted in the very image of the Creator, humanity holds a unique place in the cosmos (Genesis 1:27). This ontological truth undergirds the Christian understanding of personhood. It is not merely a biological or psychological explanation for human behavior but a theological assertion that our very essence is somehow reflective of the divine.

Moreover, this dignifying reality carries with it a heartbreaking paradox. The Genesis account illuminates not only our divine-likeness but also our inclination toward rebellion. The narrative of the Fall (Genesis 3) introduces us to Original Sin, entrenching a predisposition towards sinful behavior in the human lineage. This pivotal moment reshapes our understanding of personality and behavior, linking them inextricably to the marred propensity within us for transgression.

Within this framework, sin is not merely a litany of wrongful acts but a condition—a malady of the soul that taints our psychological makeup. It manifests in our attitudes, desires, and dispositions, warping the divine image into a spectrum of distorted likenesses. We peer through the lens of Scripture to discern not merely actions but the ripples of our fallen nature that infiltrate our consciousness and behavior (Romans 5:12).

It is an essential task for those in psychology to delve into the recesses of the psyche with an acute awareness of this intrinsic flaw. As we attempt to construct typologies that explain temperament and personality, we must do so with the recognition that each category is confounded by sin's shadow. The biblical vantage point adds not just a layer of complexity but a call for humility in our study of the human condition.

Implicit in this biblical narrative is the transformational trajectory available to humanity. Redemption through Christ (Ephesians 1:7) provides a means for humanity to transcend its inherent brokenness. This is a crucial component of any Christian anthropology; without it, our efforts to understand ourselves would be mired in despair. Instead, we can investigate the mysteries of the brain and personality with the hope of sanctification as our backdrop.

The nature of sin, as addressed in the Bible, is not merely an act but an estate from which we cannot extricate ourselves. This inherent dislocation from God's will impacts our every thought, every relationship, and every pursuit (Psalm 51:5). As a result, psychological study, when paired with a biblical worldview, must account for the pervasive effects of sin on the psyche.

Our moral failures are thus not simply instances of bad judgment but symptoms of a deeper spiritual ailment. Each thought of anger, each surge of pride, each impulse of envy reveals not just bad habits to be corrected but a soul's need for divine intervention. This is where theology and psychology converge—each disposition, each act of will can be a marker on the path leading towards or away from God's intended harmony.

Christian anthropology sees in every individual not just a biological specimen or a psychological case study, but a living soul, an image-bearer with a capacity for communion with the divine or for corruption by sin. It is this anthropology that grounds our approach in empathy and hope. The tendency toward sin is balanced by the transformative potential realized in Christ (2 Corinthians 5:17).

We must approach the study of the human psyche with the recognition that personality, as an expression of the spiritual and psychological dimensions of a person, is embroiled in a larger narrative—a drama of divine proportions. Each personal struggle reflects the universal battle between sin and grace, between decadence and redemption (Romans 7:19).

As we consider various typologies in the chapters that follow, it remains imperative to maintain this biblical perspective. The metrics and methods employed must be gauges of not just psychological patterns but of the soul's alignment with or divergence from the source of its creation and the promise of its restoration. To study personality without this cosmic backdrop is to miss the grand tapestry of divine narrative at work in each human story.

Thus, this chapter lays the groundwork for a holistic understanding of human nature, steeped in the biblical reality of creation, sin, and redemption. It underlines the essential doctrine that while sin has marred the reflection of God within us, there remains a steadfast hope offered to humanity—the rebirth of our truest selves through the redemptive work of Jesus Christ (John 3:3).

In sum, a biblical worldview equips us to approach psychological science not as an isolated discipline but as a realm deeply interwoven with spirituality and theology. It calls us to look beyond the surface of human behavior and acknowledge the spiritual dimensions at play. This perspective is not only about recognizing human brokenness but about championing the potential for divine restoration and transformation that lies within each individual.

As this chapter concludes, the path stretches before us, inviting a journey into deeper understanding. The ensuing chapters shall build upon this foundation, exploring the mappings of personality in the light of this profound and humbling truth: that our quest for self-knowledge is enveloped in a grander quest for restoration in the canvas of divine grace.

**Theological Underpinnings of Human Nature**

In the pursuit of comprehending the enigma that is human nature, we must begin by anchoring our explorations in the theological bedrock that underlies all of Christian anthropology. It is through this lens—the profound narrative of creation, fall, and redemption—that we apprehend not only the essence of humanity but also the intrinsic nature of sin that tethers the soul to its temporal struggles. Human nature, as revealed in sacred scripture, is inherently good, crafted in the imago Dei— the image of God (Genesis 1:26-27). This indelible stamp conveys the dignity and worth inherent in every human being, a reflection of the Divine that persists despite the subsequent fall from grace.

However, the original righteousness that characterized Edenic existence was marred by the advent of sin, as archetypal depicted in the narrative of Adam and Eve (Genesis 3). It is this seminal event—the willful disobedience of the protoplasts— that introduces the pernicious influence of original sin, a theological construct that elucidates the proclivity of human beings to sever communion with the Creator, and their penchant for moral turpitude. This ancestral failings' repercussions are far-reaching, permeating the collective human condition and manifesting in diverse psychological and sociological pathologies.

If one considers the treatise of Pauline scripture, particularly in the letter to the Romans (Romans 5:12-19), the apostle illuminates how through one man sin entered the world, and death through sin, thus death spread to all because all sinned. This inherent flaw is not merely an offense of religious observance, but rather a fracture in the very essence of being that distorts the faculties of the mind, the desires of the heart, and the actions of the flesh.

The dichotomy of spirit and flesh within human nature is another significant theological notion, often encapsulated in the Pauline expression of the 'old self' versus the 'new self' (Ephesians 4:22-24). The flesh, associated with sin and death, is intrinsically at odds with the spirit, which seeks communion with the Divine. This struggle is intimately known by every individual and lays a foundation for the nuanced conflict between base impulses and higher moral aspirations.

At this juncture, it is crucial to elaborate that this inherent weakness of will and disorder of desires, as articulated in the doctrine of concupiscence, is not merely an abstract theological postulate but has tangible implications for psychological discourse (Council of Trent, 1546). It is the impetus behind the proclivities and tendencies that drive human behavior—often with a propensity towards that which is contrary to our ultimate good.

To redeem this flawed condition, theological tradition affirms the indispensable role of grace—unmerited divine assistance provided for regeneration and sanctification. Grace does not obliterate human nature but rather heals, perfects, and elevates it. It operates within the intricate fabric of our psychology, realigning distorted perceptions, mending fractured wills, and restoring the imago Dei to its pristine vocation.

This theological framework of human nature necessitates a conception of the self that transcends mere material and psychological components, reaching into the realm of the spiritual and the eternal. Furthermore, sin cannot be merely categorized as errant behavior but is to be understood as rebellion against God's righteous ordinances, a disorientation of the entire human person, affecting intellect, will, and affectivity.

The biblical depiction of the human heart as 'deceitful above all things' (Jeremiah 17:9) resonates deeply within the discourse on the complexities of the human psyche. It gestures towards an understanding that our cognitive processes and emotional responses are tainted by sin, leading to a proclivity for self-deception and rationalization of iniquity.

This inherent corruption does not negate human freedom, nor does it eschew responsibility for one's actions. Instead, it proposes an intricate dance between liberum arbitrium—the freedom of choice—and the bondage of the will ensnared by sin. Thus, the journey of an individual's moral and spiritual development is a testament to the possibility of transformation through synergistic cooperation with divine grace.

Embedded within this theological context, the virtues serve as antidotes to the vices that plague the human condition. They are not merely ethical constructs but participate in divine wisdom, shaping the human person towards the good, the true, and the beautiful (CCC, 1994). In this light, virtues are both dispositions and graces that guide the person to perfect communion with God and neighbor.

Integral to this exploration is the covenantal relationship that frames the divine-human interaction. It is within this paradigm that law -- as both instruction and commandment -- is revealed not as a yoke of oppression, but as a guidepost for the flourishing of human nature (Psalm 19:7-8). Thus, obedience to divine law is not an affront to human freedom but its truest expression, aligning the human will with the Divine will.

In the ultimate analysis, the theological underpinning of human nature is inextricably linked with eschatological hope—the belief in a final restoration of all things in Christ. The present experience of human frailty and sinfulness is not the terminus of the human story, but a stage in the journey towards the beatific vision, where human nature will be fully actualized in the presence of the Divine (1 Corinthians 15:42-49).

As we progress to subsequent sections, we shall explore how these foundational theological precepts inextricably weave through the essence of original sin, the embodied reflection of the image of God in humanity, and the subsequent emergence and influence of typologies that seek to encapsulate the multi-faceted dimensions of human personality. Indeed, the interplay of these elements offers rich soil for cultivating a nuanced understanding of the human condition as envisaged in Christian revelation.

**Original Sin and Its Implications on Personality** In the preceding discourse, we have laid a foundation, emphasizing the interplay between faith and psychology. Building upon this edifice, let us now delve into the doctrine of Original Sin, its profound ramifications on human personality, and how it informs the narrative of personal transformation within a biblical worldview.

Original Sin, as asserted by Christian theology, posits that the transgression committed by the prototypical man, Adam, has cascaded through generations, staining the purity of human nature (Pederson, 1997). It is not merely an inherited guilt but a condition, a distortion of the imago Dei, thereby directly impacting the holistic construct of personality. Every individual, through this primal fracture, is born with a propensity towards sin, which influences behavior, cognition, and emotion.

This inherent flaw is not simply a minor blemish; it is an ontological rupture that disconnects humanity from its source of life and truth. It is this rupture that provides a lens through which to perceive various dimensions of personality. For instance, the proclivity of individuals to engage in conflict or suffer from anxiety can be seen not merely as psychological phenomena but as manifestations of the deeper underlying spiritual discord embedded within the human condition (Swinton, 1997).

Moreover, the concept of concupiscence, the inclination of the human heart towards evil, emerges from the doctrine of Original Sin. Concupiscence resonates within the subconscious, eliciting desires and urges that shape one's temperament. Individuals who exhibit traits of impulsivity and aggressiveness may be understood as grappling with these unconstrained impulses, which are echoes of the Original Sin festering within. The psychological constructs, when seen against the backdrop of concupiscence, garner a richer explanation, marred by theological significance.

In the struggle between flesh and spirit, the remnants of divine likeness within us compel a pursuit of virtue, even as the flesh draws us towards vice. The duality present within personality traits can be viewed through this theological dichotomy. An individual's exhibition of both altruism and selfishness reflects this internal battle ordained by the Original Sin.

The implications of Original Sin also extend to psychoanalytic perspectives, which hold that various disorders and neuroses can be attributed to repressed desires and early life experiences. The doctrine affirms that, beyond these immediate causes, there is an intrinsic distortion reverberating within the human soul, which precipitates psychological discomfort and maladaptation (Barbour, 1999).

Personality development itself, commonly understood through stages or milestones, takes on a new dimension when considering the presence of Original Sin. Each stage is not simply a psychological phase but a spiritual passage, one where the pull of innate sinfulness must be continuously overcome by the grace instilled through faith and the sacramental life.

This sin's pervasive influence cannot be contained within an individual but spills over into interpersonal relationships. The conflicts, miscommunications, and dysfunctions we observe in our dealings with 'the other' are manifested symptoms of this primal disorder. Social psychology, then, becomes not only a study of social interaction but also a commentary on the collective struggle against the residual effects of Original Sin.

In the search for self-awareness and improvement, many turn to various psychological typologies. Yet, without anchoring these in the context of Original Sin, there is a risk of superficiality. For true transformation, it is not enough to identify oneself as a particular type; one must also recognize the fallen state from which one starts and towards which divine grace beckons us to move beyond.

The trait theory asserts that personality is composed of enduring characteristics; Original Sin, too, suggests an enduring characteristic—though one deeply marred. However, while trait theory often presents personality as static, the doctrine of Original Sin offers a trajectory: from a fallen state towards redemption and sanctification (Johnson et al., 2015). This journey becomes the ultimate goal of human development within a Christian framework.

Understanding Original Sin and its implications on personality offers invaluable context for cognitive-behavioral therapies. Such therapies, which aim to reshape thought patterns and behaviors, align with the Christian narrative of repentance and conversion—a reshaping of the inner man. The sin nature, ever-present, is the substrate upon which these cognitive and behavioral modifications must be etched.

The state of fallen nature means that personality is not just a psychological construct to be measured and categorized, but a profound enigma to be understood and transformed. It involves the soul's journey towards God, the reclamation of the divine image, and the ultimate restoration of what was lost through Adam's trespass.

In conclusion, the doctrine of Original Sin elucidates how every aspect of personality is impacted by an overarching narrative of fall and redemption. Sin is not merely an external factor that disrupts human existence; it is woven into the very fabric of our being, necessitating an approach that integrates psychological understanding with theological depth.

This brings us to a critical juncture wherein the exploration of Christian Anthropology and the Image of God becomes essential, laying bare the innate dignity of the human person and the transformative power of grace that transcends the limitations imposed by Original Sin. Such an understanding is necessary to appreciate fully the complexity of personality and the potential for its redemption and flourishing within the parameters of divine truth.

**Christian Anthropology and the Image of God**

Within the Biblical worldview of humanity and sin, the concept of Christian anthropology occupies a central place. This perspective delves into the intrinsic nature of humans, created uniquely in the image of God (imago Dei). This imagery is not solely a metaphor but a foundational statement about our identity and purpose. Humanities' resemblance to the divine encompasses the spiritual, moral, rational, and relational aspects imbued within us. It is within this anthropological frame that we are to comprehend our individual and collective existence.

In the book of Genesis, we encounter the unequivocal declaration that humanity is crafted in the image and likeness of the Creator (Genesis 1:26-27). This narrative sets forth an understanding of human dignity and worth that is unparalleled. The portrayal is not of a deity distant and detached but of One who imprints on humanity a divine touch, instilling life with an eternal spark.

This theological premise asserts that each person reflects the divine attributes of God, not through physical resemblance but through capacities for creativity, reason, free will, and the ability to enter into a relationship. It is within this capability for connection that one finds the truest reflection of God—for God himself is relational, existing eternally in a communion of three persons: Father, Son, and Holy Spirit.

Christian anthropology, therefore, maintains that the essence of personhood is relational. Personality and selfhood are not developed in isolation but in communion with others and ultimately with the divine. The triune nature of God serves as a blueprint for human interactions and relationships (Pannenberg, 1991). It follows that our personalities are shaped and defined not only by our individual characteristics but also by our interactions with others and our relationships with the divine.

The fall of humanity as described in Genesis 3 introduces the fracturing of this perfect image. Sin distorts our likeness to God and disrupts the harmony of our relationships. Yet, the inherent value of every individual remains, as the image of God, though marred, is not obliterated. The journey of redemption, therefore, involves the restoration of this image within us, a task which Christianity asserts is accomplished through Christ, the perfect image of the invisible God (Colossians 1:15).

In the process of sanctification, the Holy Spirit works to transform believers more and more into the likeness of Christ (Romans 8:29), which is, in essence, the restoration of the imago Dei. The Christian life is thus marked by an ongoing renewal of the mind (Romans 12:2), reorienting our desires and actions toward the divine paradigm.

Similarly, in our study of brain organization and personality, it is essential to consider the fall and redemption narrative. Sin has affected not only our spiritual condition but our psychological and physical realities as well. Psychological disorders and maladaptive behaviors can sometimes be seen as manifestations of the broader cosmic fall. Yet, hope is found in the understanding that grace operates within these conditions, offering restoration and transformation.

The image of God in humanity also provides insights into ethics and morality. If one holds that the human person is fundamentally a reflection of the divine character, the pursuit of moral living and virtue is not arbitrary but rooted in one's very essence. Human dignity remains a non-negotiable truth that demands respect, compassion, and justice in all interpersonal endeavors.

As we continue to explore the depths of personality, it is essential to acknowledge that we are not merely products of our biology or environment but beings with an eternal destiny. The human personality is multidimensional, reflecting not just the physiological and psychological but also the spiritual reality of our existence. One's identity cannot be fully understood without recognizing the spiritual dimension that transcends material explanations.

To decipher the enigma of human personality, one must consider the narrative of creation, fall, and redemption. This narrative provides a lens through which the convolutions of human behavior and mental processes can be viewed, offering a more comprehensive understanding of the self.

Ultimately, Christian anthropology heralds a message of inherent worth and potential for every person. Regardless of the struggles one faces—be they psychological, physical, or spiritual—redemption and wholeness remain in reach. It is through this lens that psychiatrists and psychologists of faith can approach their mission, not merely as practitioners but as instruments of God's healing grace.

It must be underscored that the image of God within us allots not only unparalleled dignity but also remarkable responsibility. To live in the imago Dei is to choose to reflect divine attributes in every aspect of life, particularly in how we understand and treat others psychologically and relationally.

In conclusion, Christian anthropology provides a robust framework for understanding who we are and who we are meant to be. It speaks to our origins, our purpose, and our destiny, offering a vision of human nature that celebrates our potential to bear the divine likeness in a world fractured by sin.

**The Frameworks of Personality: A Survey**

In our journey to bridge the gap between the divine and the
empirical, we are now poised to explore the realms of
personality from both historical and contemporary vantages. Let
us, then, direct our attention to the taxonomy of personality
typologies, as they provide a scaffold upon which the
complexities of the human soul are dissected and understood.
Since antiquity, scholars and philosophers have endeavored to
capture the essence of personality, categorizing it into
typologies that reflect the multifaceted nature of human
identity.

At the inception of this scholarly pursuit, Hippocrates posited
that personality traits could be traced back to the balance of
bodily humors. His theory, though medically outdated, set a
precedent for categorizing personalities into types. Centuries
later, Jung's intricate psychological theories expanded the
groundwork, offering a system that delineates individuals into
archetypes based upon their intrinsic motivations and
unconscious predispositions (Jung, 1921).

The evolution of psychological theory has yielded a wealth of
tools designed to assess personality. From projective tests to
inventories such as the Big Five, these methodologies harness
empirical rigor to unveil the complex tapestry of human traits

(Martin, 2015). In our quest to unravel personality, we employ these tools with caution and modesty, for they are but instruments seeking to quantify the unquantifiable spirit bestowed by the Divine.

Where ancient postulations intersect with modern theory, we find the undercurrents of a profound question: Does the architecture of the human persona mirror a grander, celestial design? It is here, within this intersection, that we must wield our understanding with unwavering discernment. For the truth of personality transcends mere categorization—it echoes the imago Dei, the very image of God impressed upon us all.

In truth, historical typologies impart wisdom that transcends the epochs. The four temperaments—sanguine, phlegmatic, melancholic, and choleric—though conceived before the empirical scientific method took hold, still resonate with contemporary interpretations of personality. While the nomenclature shifts, the essence remains: human beings display a spectrum of dispositions that interact with environmental influences to shape who they are.

Contemporary typologies, in turn, offer a more systemic and data-driven approach. The Myers-Briggs Type Indicator (MBTI) and Kiersey Temperament Sorter, for instance, categorize individuals based on preferences in perception and judgment.

These modern frameworks, while not without critique, provide a window into individual cognitive styles and interpersonal dynamics (Wetzel, 1995).

It is crucial, however, to appraise these tools and typologies through the lens of a biblical worldview. We must balance the empirical findings with the wisdom of Scripture, which reveals the foundational truth about our created nature, without falling prey to the reductionism that so often pervades secular interpretations of the self.

In light of divine Revelation, we examine personality not merely as a set of traits to be measured, but as an expression of our unique calling and an invitation to virtuous living. Each typology, each framework, becomes a conversation starter, a means to delve deeper into understanding how to conform our lives more closely to that of Christ.

The endeavor to categorize personality is thus a humble recognition of our limited understanding as we aspire to know the soul, an entity breathlessly animated by the divine spark. These frameworks serve as maps that guide us through the terra incognita of the human heart, knowing full well that no earthly construct can encapsulate the breadth of God's creation within us.

As we proceed, caution must be the watchword, for it is perilously easy to mistreat these classifications as definitive markers of identity. Instead, they should be considered as helpful descriptors to foster self-awareness, personal growth, and greater empathy towards others. This is the true value of personality typologies when approached from a Christian anthropological perspective.

We must also be circumspect about the moral implications of personality assessments. The impulse to judge or typecast individuals based on a set of characteristics can be strong but must be resisted. Within the Christian community, each person's inherent worth is paramount; typologies must never be allowed to overshadow the sacred individuality bestowed by God.

Historically, the contemplation of personality has opened doors to philosophical inquiry into the nature of virtue, vice, and the soul's quest for salvation. From the summits of monastic contemplation to the rigor of the confessional, personality has been scrutinized not just for comprehension, but as a means towards spiritual progress and discipline.

Consequently, any comprehensive survey of personality frameworks must be aware of these larger implications. Those who walk in faith must use these typologies as aids in their journey towards sanctification, cognizant of the limitations and blessings inherent in such categorizations.

As this chapter traces the genealogy of personality typologies, it also invites reflection on their application within the framework of Christian anthropology. How do these schemas interact with the notions of sin, grace, and redemption as articulated in Scripture? These are the questions that must be lingered over, contemplated, and ultimately answered.

Thus, with our souls attuned to the wisdom of the Gospels and our methodologies grounded in the rigor of psychological science, we delve into the exploration and discernment of personality. In doing so, we honor both the mystery of our creation and the call to understand ourselves as God's beloved. For in every temperament, every type, there lies a pathway to greater love, deeper truth, and abiding faith.

**Historical and Contemporary Typologies**

In mapping the frameworks of personality, it is imperative that we recognize the longstanding efforts to understand the human condition which span millennia. The quest to categorize personalities is not purely a scientific endeavor, but also one deeply rooted in philosophy and theology. It begins with the ancient Greeks, who posited that human dispositions could be divided according to four bodily humors. The influence of these early typologies is still evident in contemporary models, albeit transfigured through a prism of progressive insights and divine revelation.

Within the ambit of classical typology, Hippocrates introduced the Four Humors theory, which placed individuals into sanguine, choleric, melancholic, and phlegmatic categories. This theory was predicated on the balance of bodily fluids; an imbalance was thought to influence both health and personality (Hippocrates, circa 400 B.C.). Though modern medicine has surpassed this physiological model, the Four Humors remain influential in understanding temperaments and have been woven into Christian thought as reflections of the diversity within the Body of Christ.

In parallel with the Greeks, the biblical tradition provides a rich tapestry of figures whose personalities inform our spiritual and psychological understanding. The narratives of scripture reveal types: from the contemplative wisdom of Solomon to the impulsive zeal of Peter. These scriptural archetypes exemplify the myriad ways in which personality and divine purpose intersect.

From ancient typologies, we traverse into the psychoanalytic realm with Sigmund Freud and his tripartite structure of the psyche: the id, ego, and superego (Freud, 1923). Though his work is often divergent from a Christian worldview, there remains a level of dialogue, given his recognition of the profound depths and conflicts within the human soul. This acknowledgment of inner struggle resonates with the Pauline discourse on the war between flesh and spirit.

Carl Jung further expanded the exploration of typologies by categorizing individuals based on their preferences in perceiving the world and making decisions (Jung, 1921). His delineation of introversion and extraversion, along with thinking, feeling, sensing, and intuition functions, served as precursors to later typologies like the Myers-Briggs Type Indicator, which remains widely used today.

More recent typologies have sought to contextualize personality within relational frameworks, such as the Fundamental Interpersonal Relations Orientation (FIRO-B), which examines our interpersonal needs of inclusion, control, and affection (Schutz, 1958). Within a Christian context, such models echo the intrinsic human desire for communion with God and one another, as reflected in the doctrine of the Trinity and the communal nature of the Church.

At the turn of the 21st century, the Big Five personality traits — openness, conscientiousness, extraversion, agreeableness, and neuroticism — emerged from robust empirical research as a model with wide predictive utility (Bryngelson, 1928). This scientific typology can be reconciled with Christian anthropology that affirms the inherent complexity and multifaceted nature of humans created in the image of God.

Should one venture into the therapeutic realm, they will encounter the Enneagram, a system that, despite its controversial origins, has been adopted by many within the Christian tradition as a tool for spiritual growth. Its nine interrelated personality types provide a framework for understanding the vices and virtues that align with the Beatitudes and the seven deadly sins, inviting a journey from brokenness towards holiness.

Indeed, each era has produced its own typologies, from Hans Eysenck's biologically-based personality dimensions (Eysenck, 1947) to the more recent HEXACO model emphasizing honesty-humility (White, 2016). While secular in origin, these typologies are not antithetical to faith; rather, they offer additional lenses through which to comprehend the Imago Dei.

Contemporary discourse in personality psychology often turns to the nuanced relations between genetics, environment, and agency. This triadic interplay is not foreign to those who discern the divine image within the mosaic of human freedom, original sin, and grace. It underlines the view that personality, even in its most scientifically rendered forms, can be both a reflection of the fall and a testament to divine grace working within and upon the natural order.

The integration of these historical and contemporary typologies into a comprehensive Christian psychology of personality must be done with both critical appreciation and theological discernment. It requires an understanding that while empirical research reveals aspects of the human psyche, it is theology that offers insights into the soul. The typologies derived from our faith are indispensable as they provide the moral and spiritual dimensions to our understanding of personality.

In synthesizing these typological frameworks, one must not discount the teleological aspect of personality. The Christian anthropology upholds the belief that human beings are destined for a purpose beyond themselves - a calling to participate in the divine life (Vatican II, Gaudium et Spes, 1965). Therefore, personality is not a static entity but a dynamism oriented towards the eschatological horizon where the fullness of personal vocation is realized in communion with God.

It is thus that we see personality typologies as not merely descriptive but also aspirational, guiding individuals towards the virtues that mirror the character of Christ. As new typologies arise and old ones are revisited within the context of contemporary psychology, they must be evaluated in light of our enduring faith, always considering how they can purify and elevate the reflection of God in each person.

The contemplation of personality typologies through the lens of Christian wisdom affords us not only the ability to understand others better but also beckons us to a deeper introspection of our own lives. It becomes a journey that not only categorizes traits and tendencies but also transforms our hearts to align with the divine pattern set forth in scripture, tradition, and the life of Christ Himself.

**Assessing Personality: Tools and Methodologies**

The exploration of personality is both a psychological quest and a spiritual journey, where methodologies emerge as the bridge between the observable traits and the ethereal qualities of the human spirit. The dialetic between faith and psychology rests on robust tools for assessment that respect both the material and immaterial aspects of man's nature. This chapter delves into the instruments that discern patterns within the psyche correlating to behaviors emblematic of who we are as beings created in the image of God.

When one evaluates personality, a spectrum of methodologies unveils itself, ranging from standardized tests to in-depth qualitative interviews. Among these, psychometric instruments have garnered favor for their quantifiable results and comparative analysis. These tests, while not devoid of their limitations, offer a systematic approach in examining the complexities of personality aligned with empirical science and human reason.

The Myers-Briggs Type Indicator (MBTI), for instance, provides a framework for understanding cognitive dispositions. Though its reliability and validity have been points of debate (Pittenger, 2005), many see its utility in aiding individuals to comprehend themselves and others through archetypal lenses. This instrument aligns with the teleological understanding of personality, where personal inclinations direct an individual toward their ultimate purpose.

Another widespread tool, the Five-Factor Model or Big Five, enunciates personality through openness, conscientiousness, extraversion, agreeableness, and neuroticism. The grand narrative of these factors speaks to a wider canvas of behavioral propensities that offer insights into the virtue and vice intrinsic to the human condition (McCrae & Costa, 1997).

Projective tests such as the Rorschach Inkblot Test and the Thematic Apperception Test delve deeper into the concealed corridors of the psyche, where the conscious mind often wears a veil. While these tests have been scrutinized for their subjective interpretations, they offer a contemplative approach to personality reminiscent of the reflective practices espoused within Christian tradition.

Narrative methods offer an approach much akin to the parabolic teachings of Scripture, where stories and personal accounts unveil the intricate and unique creation of each individual. Interviews, life histories, and personal narratives afford a depth of understanding that standardized tests may overlook, accommodating the subjective experience bound in the incommunicable attributes of the individual soul.

Behavioral observation stands as a mirror, reflecting the external expressions of the internal spirit in real-time. Here one can see the imprint of free will playing out, where choices made and actions taken reveal the contours of character.

Longitudinal studies extend the observational scope over the temporal expanse, offering a view into the developmental procession of personality traits. Just as the biblical narrative unfolds across generations, longitudinal methods appreciate the growth and maturing of personality over a lifetime.

Physiological measures, incorporating neuroscientific approaches, underscore the biological substrates of personality. As we unravel the linkages between brain organization and behavioral tendencies, such insights echo the unity of body and spirit as contemplated in a Christian anthropology.

However, these tools must be wielded with caution, keeping in mind that the complexity of humankind, created in the imago Dei, cannot be fully contained within psychometric scales or algorithmic formulas. Each methodology, thus, is a limited attempt to decipher the handiwork of the Divine, an exercise in humility as much as in science.

The integration of these methodologies into a coherent understanding of personality requires a baptism of sorts—a purification and synthesis through the lens of Revealed Truth.

Here, data from tools and observations are not merely processed in isolation but are contextualized within the grand narrative of redemption and grace.

No single tool or method reigns supreme; each has its merit and its place within the greater mosaic of assessment. To understand personality is to strive for a symphony of various measures, harmonized by the timeless truths that undergird the Christian faith.

This synthesis of assessment methodologies invites a contemplative discernment, one that recognizes the limitations and imperfections inherent to human inquiry. In searching the depths of personality, one must remain vigilant to the spirit behind the letter, to the essence beyond the evidence, and to the soul within the science.

As we span the breadth of personality tools, we are reminded that our assessments serve more than academic or clinical purposes—they serve the human person in their quest for self-knowledge, growth, and greater conformity to the likeness of Christ.

Thus, we proceed, armed with the best methodologies psychology offers while anchored in the wisdom of a biblical worldview. It is within this delicate balance that we seek to understand the human personality, not only to study but to edify, and not simply to categorize but to uplift.

## Chapter 3: Friedman/Rosenman's Typology Through a Biblical Lens

The investigation into the nature of humanity's complexities finds an intriguing crossroads at the intersection of Friedman and Rosenman's personality typology and biblical theology. To dissect the intricacies of the human psyche, one cannot overlook the predilections and behaviors identified by these researchers. The typology posits two predominant personality styles, Type A and Type B, each with its unique set of characteristics and implications for stress and overall health.

From a biblical standpoint, these types harbor echoes of narratives found within the Sacred Texts. Consider the quintessential sisters, Martha and Mary, whom we encounter in the narratives of the Gospel of Luke. Martha embodies the Type A personality with her industrious and hurried nature, while Mary exudes Type B traits with her contemplative and serene demeanor (Luke 10:38-42). As we delve deeper into the typology through a biblical lens, we are afforded a platform to reflect on how these personalities might balance within the framework of Scriptural wisdom.

The Type A individual is typified by a high degree of competitiveness, urgency, and aggressiveness. Characteristics that, if left unchecked, may give rise to sin in the form of anger, envy, or pride. In contrast, the biblical injunctions advocate for moderation, humility, and patience (Galatians 5:22-23). The challenge, then, is to reconcile the Type A proclivities with the virtues extolled throughout the Scriptures.

Conversely, Type B personalities are often portrayed as more relaxed, less competitive, and more reflective. These are attributes that align closely with the biblical calls to contemplation and gentleness. However, it's also noted that sloth and indifference are warned against in biblical teaching, thereby providing a caution to those of the Type B disposition against complacency (Proverbs 6:6-11).

Stress is a pervasive element in the narrative of Type A individuals. The urgency and hassle that highlight their existence find little refuge in the serenity prescribed by Scripture. It is through the lens of sin and its consequences that stress can be viewed not only as a psychological phenomenon but also as a spiritual malaise. The biblical prescription to cast all our anxieties on God speaks directly into this turmoil, offering a path to transcendence (1 Peter 5:7).

The management of stress for Type A individuals can indeed be framed as a spiritual discipline. Self-control, a fruit of the Spirit, becomes a crucial attribute for the Type A individual to cultivate (Galatians 5:22-23). Acknowledgment of human limitations and the embrace of divine sovereignty can lead to a more peaceful existence, mitigating the physiological perils associated with chronic stress.

Type B personalities, on the other hand, may find that their more relaxed approach to life resonates with the biblical counsel to live in contentment and trust in God's providence (Philippians 4:11-13). Yet, the Type B person must guard against the spiritual malady of indolence. The biblical ethos calls for a balanced life, one that values both rest and active engagement in one's vocations.

As we contextualize the Friedman/Rosenman model within a Christian perspective, it becomes apparent that the typology is more than a mere psychological construct; it serves as a mirror reflecting our sinful tendencies and the redemptive possibilities available through a life aligned with biblical principles (Romans 7:18-24).

Indeed, Scripture does not exclude the tendencies described by Friedman and Rosenman but provides a larger narrative into which these personalities must find their place. The biblical figure Paul, for instance, could be viewed as a redeemed Type A character, harnessing his zeal and energy for the cause of Christ (Acts 9). Ruth, with her steady and gentle devotion, might be considered as exemplifying Type B traits within a redemptive context (Ruth 1-4).

Both personality types, within the biblical portrait of humanity, must contend with the universal human struggle against sin and the ongoing process of sanctification. For the Christian, transformation is a lifelong process, and personality traits are subject to the renewing work of the Holy Spirit (Romans 12:2).

The virtues prescribed in Scripture thus serve as the antidote to the excesses of both personality types. The Type A individual is called to embrace patience, peace, and service, while the Type B is encouraged towards diligence, passion, and resolve.

This perspective not only affirms the validity of psychological study but deeply enriches it by providing eternal context. It posits that our personalities are not static entities but dynamic parts of our being that can be sanctified and redeemed (2 Corinthians 5:17).

In closing, as we reflect upon Friedman and Rosenman's typology through a biblical lens, we find a poignant reminder of the human condition and the transformative power of grace. Personality, viewed in this light, becomes a dimensional facet of our journey toward holiness, informed by Scripture and consecrated by faith.

**Type A and Type B Personalities: The Balance of Martha and Mary**

The dichotomy of Type A and Type B personalities, first delineated by Friedman and Rosenman, provides an intriguing framework for exploring human temperament from a biblical perspective. In understanding Martha and Mary, two sisters in the Gospel of Luke, we encounter a profound embodiment of these typologies. Martha, often associated with Type A traits, is absorbed in tasks and the bustling management of her duties, while Mary, reflecting Type B attributes, is depicted as contemplative and present, focused on the deeper relational aspect of life (Luke 10:38-42). This section explores the significance of both personality types within the context of the Christian understanding of personhood.

The Type A personality, characterized by a driven, competitive, and impatient nature, finds its resonance in Martha's predisposition. The seeking of excellence and, at times, the wrestling with anxiety, are aspects that can indeed be spiritually fruitful yet may also be stumbling blocks to the tranquility of the soul. Type B individuals, on the other hand, often personified through the calm and reflective Mary, exhibit a pronounced inclination toward peace and relational depth. These characteristics, though they provide a foundation for spiritual richness, may also contribute to a lack of urgency in the temporal realm (Friedman & Rosenman, 1974).

From a Christian anthropological perspective, neither Type A nor Type B personalities are fixed nor entirely defining of one's character. Rather, they are both reflections of the Image of God, illuminating diverse facets of the Creator's nature – His meticulous order and His immeasurable capacity for relationship. The narrative of Martha and Mary invites believers to recognize the inherent good in varied temperaments, suggesting that each has its place in the Kingdom of God (Genesis 1:27).

Integration of the typological characteristics into one's life must be handled with discernment. For the Type A individual, the virtues of diligence, determination, and responsibility may be harnessed without succumbing to the vices of excessive worry or domineering behaviors. The art lies in embodying the spiritual discipline of moderation, where one's vigorous nature yields fruit without overwhelming one's peace (Proverbs 4:23).

Equally, Type B individuals are called to cultivate their natural propensity for tranquility and relational depth, ensuring that their peaceable nature does not slip into indolence or passivity. The biblical exhortation to be 'as wise as serpents and as innocent as doves' becomes significant here, as it encourages the tempering of serenity with the wisdom of action when necessity dictates (Matthew 10:16).

The interaction between Martha and Jesus underscores the necessity of balancing activity with contemplation. Jesus does not reprimand Martha for her service but rather invites her to prioritize – highlighting that Mary's choice to listen and learn was essential in that moment. This presents a paradigm wherein the Martha's of the world can acknowledge the value in the Mary archetype, a realization of the 'better part,' the one that won't be taken away (Luke 10:42).

Within this scriptural account, a metaphor for Christian living emerges, advocating a harmonious personality that encapsulates the strengths of both Martha and Mary. The challenge is to craft a life where one can attend to the exigencies of the mundane without losing sight of the eternal and the sacred. Herein lies the heart of Christian vocation, which directs one to action infused with prayer and contemplation.

The balance seeks not to eliminate the natural inclinations of the individual but to perfect them through grace, such that Type A's dynamism aligns with God's purpose, and Type B's peacefulness does not become complacency but an invitation to divine encounter (2 Peter 1:5-8).

This balanced approach requires profound self-knowledge. It is here that the psychological tool of personality assessment can serve as a handmaid to spiritual growth when wielded with wisdom. Through understanding one's inherent tendencies, one can better align their natural gifts with God's will, a process akin to the refinement of silver through fire (Proverbs 17:3).

A critical examination of the Type A and Type B framework within the Christian ethos illuminates not only the traits of the individual but also the dynamic nature of sanctification. The spiritual journey is marked by a progressive conforming to the image of Christ, who embodies the fullness of every virtuous trait – He is both the ultimate servant and the one who is fully present with the Father (John 14:10).

The ecclesial community provides the context in which these personality types can be nurtured and brought to full expression. The Body of Christ is composed of many members, each with different functions and qualities, and it is through this diversity that the church finds its unity and strength (1 Corinthians 12:12-27).

The biblical exploration of personality types is not a path to rigid categorization. Instead, it is a gateway to understanding the complex nature of human beings, created uniquely and called to live in a manner that reflects the diversity and unity of the Trinity. A balance must be struck – a synthesis of action and contemplation that respects individual temperaments while urging each toward the common goal of sanctification.

Type A and Type B personalities, as represented by Martha and Mary, offer a comprehensive view of human attributes and capabilities. The call is not to denigrate or prefer one over the other but to recognize the value of both and the manner in which they can be sanctified and integrated for the greater glory of God. It is a call toward wholeness – an acknowledgment that full human flourishing is found in the embrace of both the contemplative and the active life, directed towards the divine.

As such, the biblical stories continue to serve as a compass, guiding believers in the understanding and embodiment of their God-given nature. Martha and Mary are not just figures from the past; they are present in the psychological makeup of each individual, inviting an ongoing reflection on the way one inhabits their personality and engages with the world.

The examination of Type A and Type B personalities through a biblical lens provides a profound hermeneutic for self-understanding and growth in virtue. It illuminates the path to recognizing not only one's predispositions but also the means by which these traits can be harmonized with a life of faith, hope, and love, pointing ever towards the transcendent, towards communion with the Divine.

## Stress, Sin, and Salvation: Integrating Biblical Concepts

In exploring the intricate interplay between stress, sin, and salvation through the prism of the biblical worldview, it is imperative to understand that human existence is navigated within the tension of our fallen nature and the redemptive work of Christ. This dynamic paradigm, when examined through the lens of Friedman/Rosenman's typology, provides a unique framework for discerning the spiritual dimensions underlying our psychological predispositions.

The propensity for individuals to gravitate towards Type A characteristics—competitiveness, urgency, and aggression—can be seen as a manifestation of the inner turmoil caused by sin. Here, sin is not merely a set of wrongful acts, but a pervasive condition that affects the entire being (Romans 7:18-19). The relentless pursuit and unremitting stress that typify Type A behavior may reflect a deeper spiritual restlessness, a soul yearning for peace and completeness apart from God (Augustine, 400/2009).

In contrast, Type B individuals, displaying tranquility, patience, and a laid-back attitude, may embody an aspect of the biblical exhortation to "Be still, and know that I am God" (Psalm 46:10, NIV). Nevertheless, a Type B disposition is not immune to sin's influence. Sloth, disguised as relaxation, or indifference masked as contentment, can just as readily derail one's spiritual journey (Proverbs 6:6-11).

Stress, viewed through scriptural teaching, is not inherently sinful; it is a natural response to life's challenges. Jesus Christ himself experienced stress, most poignantly in the garden of Gethsemane (Luke 22:44). Yet in His stress, there was no sin; it became an avenue for complete obedience to the Father's will (Hebrews 4:15).

The Biblical narrative unearths that stress becomes sinful when it leads us to trust in our own strength rather than in divine providence. When the burdens of life accrue, and the yoke becomes heavy, the scripture invites us to exchange it for the lightness of Christ's yoke, which promises rest for our souls (Matthew 11:28-30).

The interaction between stress and sin conveys a profound implication for salvation. The state of stress can catalyze a recognition of our own insufficiency and propel us toward the salvific grace of God. It is through the acknowledgment of our inability to save ourselves that we are drawn to the Savior, who offers the ultimate resolution to our restlessness (Ephesians 2:8-9).

Salvation, therefore, does not eradicate stress but transforms our response to it. In Christ, we are gifted with a peace that surpasses all understanding (Philippians 4:7), capable of guiding our hearts even amidst turmoil. This peace, divinely infused, fosters resilience and equanimity, as the Holy Spirit aids believers in developing fruits contrary to the sinful nature of stress (Galatians 5:22-23).

Integrating Friedman/Rosenman's typology with biblical teaching, we discern that the typology does not merely categorize behaviors but can serve as a diagnostic tool revealing the soul's cry for redemption. Individuals possessing Type A tendencies may need to seek solace in the presence of God, learning from Mary's posture at Jesus' feet—an attitude of serene attentiveness (Luke 10:39-42).

Type B individuals, in turn, are called to engage actively with their faith, ensuring that their seemingly inherent peace fosters purposeful action rather than complacency. The balance of Martha and Mary becomes pivotal here, affirming that service and contemplation are not dichotomous but complementary within the Christian life (Luke 10:38-42).

Friedman and Rosenman's typology, when seen through the matrix of sin and salvation, reveals the need for personal examination and sanctification. One must be conscientious not to let Type A attributes lead to pride and self-reliance, nor should Type B traits seduce one into indifference or inaction (Proverbs 16:18, James 2:17).

The integration of this typology within the biblical context illuminates the redemptive potential that stress may hold. It is not the eradication of stress but its consecration that we should pursue. Stress sanctified by grace becomes a vehicle for spiritual growth and a reminder of our reliance on God's power made perfect in weakness (2 Corinthians 12:9).

It is evident that an authentic Christian anthropology recognizes the complex interplay of psychological typologies with the entropic effects of sin and the transformative journey toward salvation. Integration of these dimensions is not solely for the cultivation of personal holiness but is instrumental in the broader witness of the Church to a world grappling with stress and searching for meaning.

The insights gleaned from these intersections are not meant to be conclusive, but rather serve as a starting point for ongoing reflection and dialogue within the Christian community. The pursuit of understanding the human soul in its entirety is a reflection of the divine image in our quest for knowledge and wisdom (Colossians 2:2-3).

In conclusion, the dance between stress, sin, and salvation, as analyzed through the distinct but interconnected lives of Type A and Type B personalities, beckons us to a deeper understanding of our own identities in light of Christ's redemptive work. By embracing the biblical perspective, we can navigate the complexities of human nature with a clarity that is grounded in eternal truth.

**FIRO-B and the Need for Connection in Scripture**

The fundamental quest for understanding one's place within a
community is deeply rooted in the human psyche. This pursuit
of connection, articulated through the FIRO-B theory developed
by William Schutz, intersects with the scriptural beckoning
towards communion with one another and with the Divine. The
FIRO-B, standing for Fundamental Interpersonal Relations
Orientation-Behavior, offers a prism through which the Biblical
call for inclusion, control, and affection can be viewed with fresh
eyes.

The essence of inclusion within the Biblical narrative is not
confined to mere participation but reflects a profound belonging
to a people set apart (Kierkegaard et al., 1995). The Acts of the
Apostles, for instance, depicts the early church as a community
distinguished by its radical inclusivity, breaking bread with a
unity of purpose and heart. This scriptural practice embodies
the FIRO-B element of inclusion, nurturing the psychological
need for belonging through spiritual kinship.

Control in FIRO-B speaks of influence and leadership, a theme
bound to scriptural narrative wherein individuals are called to
stewardship and governance. Consider the wisdom of Proverbs
that speaks of guidance and authority (Proverbs 11:14),

paralleling Schutz's delineation of decision-making roles and their contribution to group stability and direction.

Affection, the third strand of FIRO-B's triad, resonates with the biblical command to love one another intimately as Christ has loved (John 13:34-35). This scriptural enjoinment can be conceptualized as the fulfillment of the interpersonal need for closeness and warmth within relationships, ensuring affection is not simply an emotional response but a defining relational characteristic.

One may observe the synchronization of the FIRO-B dimensions with Paul's illustration of the church as the body of Christ. In his first epistle to the Corinthians, Paul speaks of the diversity of gifts and roles yet emphasizes the unity and interdependence of each member for the proper functioning of the body (1 Corinthians 12:12-27). Such analogies are tributaries feeding into the larger stream of a biblical understanding of community, which embraces inclusion, exercises holy control, and cherishes divine affection.

FIRO-B's facets serve as a vessel for comprehending the complexity of biblical relationships, from the intimacy between David and Jonathan to the structures of leadership that Moses established. As we delve into the tapestry of bonds that constitute our religious ancestry, we witness a perennial need for connection that aligns with the psychosocial constructs like that of Schutz's.

In further developing this thought, one might contemplate Christ's modelling of leadership as being servant-hearted, an inversion of the world's understanding of control. Mark's Gospel presents Jesus redefining greatness as servitude (Mark 10:42-45), asserting that genuine control within the Christian context embodies humility and service more than power or authority.

The Biblical approach to inclusion advocates for an outreach that transcends societal boundaries. Jesus' discourse with the Samaritan woman at the well (John 4:7-26) challenges the prejudiced segregations of the time, reinforcing inclusion that surpasses ethnic, gender, and cultural divides.

This divine affection is illustrated profoundly in moments such as Jesus' weeping over Lazarus (John 11:35), where the empathetic bond and deep concern showcase a divine model of interpersonal affection. Such a depiction calls for believers to foster relationships grounded in empathy and genuine care, mirroring the heavenly pattern.

Therefore, FIRO-B, as a psychological construct, can be an instrumental lens through which scripture elucidates the conception of human relational needs. Its principles echo the divine ordination that mankind is built not for isolation but for fellowship; not for dominance but for compassionate stewardship; not for detached interactions but for loving engagement.

The empirical evidence for FIRO-B's efficacy in examining groups (Schutz, 1958) fortifies the notion that our relational needs are indeed an integral part of the human design. Such considerations grant a more nuanced understanding of how these needs are not only psychologically valid but also theologically consistent and desirable.

Within the Christian community, the assessment and appreciation of each individual's need for inclusion, control, and affection can foster a healthier body of believers. By acknowledging these intrinsic desires, the church can work towards creating an environment where each member feels valued, has a sense of purpose, and experiences the warmth of Christian fellowship.

In conclusion, the intersection of FIRO-B's outline of fundamental interpersonal relations with biblical teachings illuminates the scriptural underpinning of human relational needs. It enhances our appreciation of the divine impetus towards the establishment of a community that embodies the qualities of inclusion, stewardship, and affection grounded in love which is the very nature of God.

## Inclusion, Control, and Affection in Biblical Relationships

As we delve into the fabric of the scriptural narrative, a pattern emerges regarding how relationships are woven through the need for inclusion, control, and affection. These elements, as we have seen within the FIRO-B model—Fundamental Interpersonal Relations Orientation-Behavior—are intrinsic to the human experience. The scriptural portrayal of relationships lays bare this intrinsic relational triad, reminding us that such needs are not merely psychological constructs but echo the intricate design of Divine intent.

Inclusion is the first spoke in this triad, and its importance is emphasized throughout scripture. Beginning in Genesis, Adam is provided a companion in Eve, indicating that human beings are not designed to navigate existence in solitude (Genesis 2:18). The body of Christ metaphor in 1 Corinthians 12 articulates a vision for the church where each member belongs and possesses a specific function. This inclusion is not based on status or capability but on the inherent worth gifted by creation itself.

Control, or influence within relationships and environment, emerges as a biblical theme when we examine the stewardship entrusted to humanity. Adam's dominion over the garden (Genesis 1:28) and Moses' leadership of Israel (Exodus 3-4) illustrate the scriptural sanctioning of control—albeit a type that is accountable and servant-hearted. In the New Testament, Jesus teaches his disciples about the true nature of leadership and control: not as tyranny, but as humble service (Mark 10:42-45).

Affection, the warmth and closeness between individuals, is a relational need starkly depicted in the Bible. The deep friendship between David and Jonathan (1 Samuel 18:1-3) and Jesus' love for his disciples (John 13:1) are testaments to the divine valuation of affection. They illustrate that affection is not a mere human sentiment but a reflection of God's own relational nature.

Consider, as well, the Church's nascent days, when members pooled resources and shared lives in an effort to meet each other's needs for inclusion, control, and affection (Acts 2:42-47). This community living did not only demonstrate sacrificial love but reinforced every believer's sense of belonging, their role, and their emotional bonds.

In scripture, relational breakdowns often occur when these three needs are not met or are misunderstood. Absalom's rebellion against David (2 Samuel 15) can be discerned through a lens of unmet needs for control and inclusion. In the opposite direction, Solomon's excessive need for affection led to his spiritual downfall (1 Kings 11).

However, redemption of these needs is possible and demonstrated in the restoration of broken relationships. The return of the Prodigal Son (Luke 15:11-32), where inclusion and affection are extended without prerequisite, highlights the grace-filled potential of human connections. The father extends unmerited inclusion and affection to the erring son, symbolizing God's welcoming love.

Even the principles articulated in the epistles such as 'bearing one another's burdens' (Galatians 6:2) and 'being subject to one another out of reverence for Christ' (Ephesians 5:21), can be viewed within the context of meeting these essential relational needs in a manner that glorifies God.

If we contemplate the Last Supper (John 13), we witness Jesus instilling a new paradigm: washing the feet of his disciples as an expression of inclusive servanthood, transforming notions of control, and sharing a meal that deepens communal ties hence, affection.

From this investigation, it is apparent that the biblical record does not merely acknowledge the human need for inclusion, control, and affection; it validates and elevates it. The triune God, within Himself, displays perfect inclusion, control, and affection—an archetype that humanity aspires to reflect.

Therefore, in addressing the depth of these needs, scripture does not simply outline a series of relational duties; it unveils a pattern of divine origin. It is a pattern that calls individuals into a transformative process—reshaping natural inclinations towards inclusion, control, and affection to mirror divine qualities.

As we integrate these scriptural insights with the psychological understandings from FIRO-B, we observe a convergence of human and divine relational wisdom. Perhaps this relational dynamic, so fundamental to human thriving, was ingrafted in the soul at creation, allowing for an innate cognition between God's relational attributes and the relational dynamics of humanity.

In summation, the scriptural approach to relationships viewed through the prism of the FIRO-B framework reaffirms these core needs as deeply spiritual and intrinsically human. It provides a theological affirmation that the desire for inclusion, control, and affection are not to be shunned as worldly, but embraced as gateways to understanding God's interrelational design for humanity.

**The Church as the Body: Interpersonal Dynamics and Divine Design**

In exploring the interplay between established psychological theory and biblical exegesis, our cogitations must assimilate the precepts of the church elucidated within the sacred scriptures. Delving into the FIRO-B theory elucidates a profound hunger for connection intrinsic to human nature. The church, as the universal body, epitomizes this relational dynamic through its structural embodiment of divine intent. Such an interpretation harmonizes with not only our deepest psychological cravings but also with the divine design—a tableau of unity reflecting the Trinitarian archetype (Van Kooten, 2023).

The church's conception as a multiplicity of members, yet one body, delineates a divinely orchestrated ecosystem of interpersonal dynamics. Each part, deemed indispensable, assumes a distinct role commensurate with the gifts bestowed by the Spirit. The apostle's delineation of gifts within the body (1 Corinthians 12:12-27) resonates with the nuanced appreciation that individual variability serves the comprehensive organism, underscoring inclusion, control, and affection in harmonious execution.

Observations by modern psychology assert that inclusion within a group is a primal need, and the early church's practice of breaking bread and communal living paints a portrait of this inclusion at its zenith (Acts 2:46-47). This collective journey aligns with the psychological imperative for belonging and highlights a profound congruence with the FIRO-B model in a scriptural context.

Control, as articulated in FIRO-B, is not depicted as authoritarianism within the church's anatomy but as a shared stewardship with Christ as the sovereign head. The divine blueprint allocates equilibrium between leadership and servitude (Ephesians 4:15-16), fostering a milieu where authority is exercised in symbiosis with humility and mutual edification.

Affection, the third component of FIRO-B, finds its express representation in the 'one another' commandments sprawling throughout the New Testament. The edicts to love, serve, and encourage one another (John 13:34, Galatians 5:13, 1 Thessalonians 5:11) are not mere moral imperatives but existential necessities for the spiritual vitality of the cohesive body.

The relational architecture of the church, as ordained in scripture, not only corroborates the psychological underpinnings exemplified by FIRO-B but also bears witness to a schema that eclipses human design. This complex interplay of relationships, functioning in consonance, heeds an orchestrated symphony—a liturgy that reverberates the heartbeat of creation (Colossians 3:14).

Indeed, the church's intrinsic nature as the body of Christ supersedes purely transactional relationships and cements its foundation in agape love—a selfless, sacrificial love that empowers its members to surpass their individual limitations and forge a collective strength (1 John 4:8).

Moreover, the psychological comfort found in being understood and accepted within the body is paralleled by the overarching grace that envelops the believer. In such sanctified communion, the facets of individual personality and propensity are not obliterated but sanctified and channeled towards the common good (Romans 12:4-5).

It is essential to recognize that the church's unity does not necessitate uniformity. The manifestation of diverse gifts and services is intended not for dissonance but for a harmonious complexity, which reflects the multifaceted wisdom of God (Ephesians 3:10).

In this divine design, the barriers erected by sin—pride, envy, and malice—are systematically dismantled by the ethos of the church modeled on the principles of inclusion, control, and affection. This model serves not only to enhance social cohesion but to fulfill the divine mandate of reflecting God's glory as his image-bearers in the world (2 Corinthians 3:18).

The orchestration of the church body, therefore, is neither haphazard nor solely human-conceived, but a direct reflection of divine wisdom. Each member's role and relation serve as integral threads in the tapestry woven by God's own hand (Ephesians 2:10).

As such, the psychosocial construct of the church can be seen as a living entity, continually growing and being perfected in love. This dynamic process also parallels the sanctification journey of each believer, wherein transformation is perpetrated through relational integrity and a consistent alignment with the divine will (Philippians 1:6).

In conclusion, the church as the body is not an archaic metaphor but a living testament to the reality of our created purpose and destiny. It is within this divine tapestry that the need for connection—so deeply woven into the fabric of our being—finds its ultimate expression and fulfillment (Hebrews 10:24-25).

In surveying the congregation of believers, one cannot help but behold the sublime interaction of separate parts collaborating in a higher order. It is through such observation that we comprehend the sophistication of the church as more than a mere human institution, but rather, a celestial prototype manifested on earth.

Finally, in recognizing our place within the body, we assimilate an experiential knowledge that surpasses intellectual assent. It is in the active participation of love, service, and communal life that we not only understand our role within the church but embody the principles of divine design—testaments to an immaculate psychology (1 Peter 4:10).

**Chapter 5: Hippocrates' Four Humors and the Temperaments of the Bible**

Amidst the discourse on faith and psychology, one finds Hippocrates' doctrine of the four humors, a theory that offers insights even amidst modern advancements. As we explore these ancient insights, it is essential to discern their relevance to scriptural teachings and the nature of humanity from a Christian perspective. The four classical humors — sanguine, choleric, melancholic, and phlegmatic — were believed by Hippocrates to be the cornerstone of health and temperament. Each humor correlates to a natural element and to particular personality traits that resonate through the seminal texts of the biblical narrative.

For example, the sanguine temperament, linked to the blood, is characterized by a buoyant, optimistic, and social personality. When we gaze upon the narratives of David's musicianship and celebration in the presence of the Ark (2 Samuel 6:14-15), or Mary Magdalene's effervescent faith at the empty tomb (John 20:16), we can't help but see reflections of this sanguine fervor, with its roots deep in the human psyche (Zuckerman, 1991).

Conversely, the choleric individual is more akin to the yellow bile, signifying a passionate, ambitious, and sometimes aggressive demeanor. The determination of Nehemiah rebuilding the walls (Nehemiah 4:6) and the apostle Paul's relentless missionary journeys (Acts 16:10) exemplify the dynamic and purpose-driven attributes of the choleric temperament (Mondak et al., 2008).

The melancholic humor, tied to black bile, can be seen as synonymous with thoughtful, analytical, and often somber individuals. Consider the introspective nature of Solomon in Ecclesiastes (Ecclesiastes 1:2) or the lamentations of Jeremiah (Lamentations 3:1). These sacred texts mirror the depth and existential contemplation that characterizes the melancholic disposition (Dana, 2000).

In contrast, the phlegmatic temperament, associated with phlegm, is emblematic of calm, reliable, and compassionate personas. We see this in the gentle strength of Joseph, a provider of refuge in the time of famine (Genesis 41:36), and in the nurturing care of Martha, offering hospitality to Jesus (Luke 10:40). These personalities embody the steadiness of the phlegmatic humor (Phipps, 2012).

It is quite fascinating to see how these temperaments, codified by Hippocrates, have permeated throughout history, influencing the study of psychology and echoing in the lives of the biblical figures. It is within this interplay of ancient wisdom and divine revelation that we can derive a deeper understanding of the human condition.

However, it is crucial to approach these humors not as deterministic but as frameworks that provide an informative lens to assess character. They do not confine individuals to rigid categories but rather invite a fuller exploration of the complexities within God's creation. As such, the humors can be viewed as foundational elements, which, combined with divine grace, contribute to the unique manifestation of each person's spirit (Aquinas, Summa Theologica, Question 77, Article 1, Reply to Objection 3).

The application of the four humors has evolved over time. While contemporary psychology has advanced beyond the humoral theory in terms of empirical research, the conceptual essence of these temperaments persists in modern personality assessments. The enduring nature of these typologies underscores their intrinsic value in understanding human behavior (Galen, c. 200 AD/1968).

This ongoing relevance also manifests in the interaction between these temperaments and Christian virtues. For instance, the virtue of fortitude may align with the dynamism of the choleric, while prudence resonates with the contemplative depth of the melancholic. It is the synthesis of these temperaments with virtues that shapes a Christian's journey towards holiness, acknowledging both their humoral predispositions and their calling in Christ.

In viewing these temperaments through the lens of scriptural revelation, one acknowledges the role of divine providence in shaping character traits. The Bible presents diverse personalities, each with their strengths and weaknesses, as an ensemble of humanity redeemed through grace. The temperaments are not markers of destiny; rather, they illustrate the varied canvas upon which God's grace operates.

The concept of humors also finds resonance in the principle of balance, which parallels biblical teachings on temperance and moderation. The physical and spiritual equilibrium depicted in scripture (Philippians 4:5) can be likened to the holistic balance of the humors, where an excess or deficiency reflects a disordered state, be it of body or soul.

While Hippocrates' four humors provide a schema for understanding different dispositions, it is within the narratives of scripture that one finds the ultimate guidance for living a life characterized by balance, virtue, and grace. It is this balance that informs the Christian's response to life's vicissitudes, tempered by the wisdom of God's Word.

It is paramount to engage with these concepts, not merely as historical artifacts but as touchstones in the pursuit of an integrated approach to psychology within a Christian framework. The humors serve as a reminder of the need for equilibrium, an equilibrium that is not only physiological but also spiritual in nature.

In the final analysis, the integration of Hippocrates' four humors with biblical temperaments encourages an enriched dialogue between faith and psychology. It extends an invitation to embrace the breadth of human diversity within the divine tapestry, recognizing the uniqueness and dignity of each individual as a masterpiece in progress.

Perhaps, in this exploration, one discovers not only a psychological typology but also, at a deeper level, a reflection of the divine imprint upon the human soul—a theme that continues to unfold in the subsequent chapters of this work, marrying the wisdom of antiquity with the timeless truths of the Bible.

**Sanguine, Choleric, Melancholic, and Phlegmatic
Personalities in Scripture**

Within the Scriptures, a rich tapestry of personalities is
discernible, characters whose traits mirror the sanguine,
choleric, melancholic, and phlegmatic temperaments described
by Hippocrates. These temperaments provide unique lenses
through which we may view Biblical figures, understanding
them not merely as historical entities but as archetypes of
human behavior and divine interaction (Galen, 2nd century).

Consider the sanguine personality, often marked by a buoyant,
social, and charismatic nature. In scripture, we may see this
temperament in the figure of King David, a man of passion,
artistic talent, and leadership. His Psalms resonate with a zest
for life and deep personal relationships, a hallmark of the
sanguine disposition (I Samuel 16). Peter, too, can be viewed
through a sanguine perspective; his impulsive acts, like stepping
onto the water to meet Jesus, reveal a sanguine's adventurous
spirit (Matthew 14:29).

The choleric temperament, known for its assertive, determined,
and often aggressive qualities, can be seen in Paul the Apostle.
Paul's fervent preaching and tireless work exhibit the drive and
ambition characteristic of the choleric type. His dramatic
conversion and subsequent missionary journeys reflect a

personality inclined toward leadership and reform (Acts 9:1-19).

In contrast, the melancholic temperament is reflective, analytical, and sensitive. Jeremiah, the "weeping prophet," who lamented his sufferings and the tribulations of his people, embodies this personality. His introspection and concern for righteousness are intrinsic to the temperament's thoughtful and conscientious nature (Jeremiah 9:1).

The phlegmatic personality, calm, reliable, and thoughtful, may be seen in Joseph, the earthly father of Jesus. His steady protection of Mary and the newborn Jesus, his quiet decision-making, and his unwavering faith in God's messages through dreams demonstrate the phlegmatic's tranquil and supportive demeanor (Matthew 1:19-25).

The concept of temperaments can be perceived not simply as a psychological construct but as an expression of the divine image within humanity. Each temperament, with its strengths and weaknesses, can be seen as a pathway to holiness and a reflection of the Imageo Dei when aligned with virtue and governed by grace (Genesis 1:27).

Indeed, the scriptures do not merely allow us to classify these individuals; they encourage us to see how each temperament, when directed towards God's will, can serve the Kingdom in various capacities. The impulsive Peter became the "rock" upon which the Church was built, demonstrating that a sanguine's adaptability and fervor can be harnessed for profound leadership (Matthew 16:18).

Similarly, Paul's choleric intensity was redeemed from persecution to proclamation, showing that determined vigor, when redeemed, is invaluable in the work of evangelization and church planting (Galatians 1:23).

The reflective depth of the melancholic Jeremiah produced writings that offer not just lamentations but hope and a call to repentance. His emotional sensitivity became a conduit for expressing God's passionate love for His people (Jeremiah 31:3).

Joseph's phlegmatic steadfastness provided the Holy Family's earthly foundation, suggesting that contemplative peace and stability are integral to nurturing the divine gifts entrusted to our care (Luke 2:51-52).

As we examine these temperaments within the Biblical narrative, we see that each trait can be a source of virtue or vice, depending on its master. A sanguine temperament left unchecked may drift towards superficiality or promiscuity, just as a choleric might towards cruelty or domination. The melancholic may succumb to despondence, and the phlegmatic to sloth or complacency (Galen, 2nd century).

Yet conversely, when these humors are subjected to divine grace, what transformation occurs! The sanguine's warmth becomes the fire of charity, the choleric's ambition the catalyst for justice. The melancholic's depth turns to wisdom, and the phlegmatic's stability anchors the tumultuous sea of change (Aquinas, 13th century).

Thus, the dynamics of these temperaments serve not just as psychological insights but as spiritual exhortations. They are integrally linked with the Biblical exhortation to "put on the new self, created to be like God in true righteousness and holiness" (Ephesians 4:24 NIV).

These personalities in scripture offer a means to introspect and identify, to view our own tendencies in the light of God's redemptive touch. They provide a context for understanding how our unique design can serve His purpose and His people.

In conclusion, these humors remind us that in the breadth of divine creation, variety serves unity in the body of Christ. Sanguine or melancholic, choleric or phlegmatic - each temperament becomes a testament to the imago Dei when it aligns with the character of Christ. And just as the body consists of many parts, so too does the Church prosper in the harmonious function of its diverse members (1 Corinthians 12:12-14).

**Historical Perspectives and Modern Applications**

Immersed in tradition yet ceaselessly advancing, modern applications of the Hippocratic theory of the four humors refract through the prismatic lens of contemporary psychology, yielding insights that harmonize with scriptural teachings about human temperament. Even as prevailing medical doctrine has transcended these ancient classifications, their metaphysical parallels persist in exploring the canvas of human disposition through a biblical frame. The interplay between these venerable perspectives and today's approaches invites an incisive inquiry into the temperaments of the Bible, contemplating their reach beyond mere physiological explanation.

The ancient Greek physicians contemplated the essence of humans through a quartet of humors: blood, yellow bile, black bile, and phlegm. This perspective, attributed to the age of Hippocrates, professed that the balance among these substances was pivotal for health, both physical and psychological (Rouhiainen, 2020). The humors were thought to correspond with seasonal changes and elements in nature, an echo of the deeply interconnected worldview held by early scholars and theologians.

From this quartet arose the temperaments: sanguine, choleric, melancholic, and phlegmatic. Fast forward through the centuries, and these temperaments have been revisited through the application of personality typologies within biblical contexts. Current interpretations often look at these humors less as biological fluids and more as symbolic descriptions of personality traits that resonate with scriptural characters and teachings, providing believers with models for understanding and reflecting upon their own nature.

The sanguine temperament, traditionally associated with blood, is paralleled with vivacious and sociable biblical figures. Invariably, this correlates with the invitational and communal strategies endorsed by scriptures, suggesting a deity-designed predilection towards relationality within the human estate. The modern understanding of the sanguine temperament emphasizes its innate strength in connectivity, which aligns with the Christian exhortation to love and fellowship (Rouhiainen, 2020).

Choleric individuals, construed from yellow bile, resonate with the assertive and leadership-driven personalities witnessed in the annals of scripture. Leaders like Moses, with a fierce commitment to divine directives, embody this temperament. Modern discourse recognizes the utility of such driven individuals in positions of influence and decision-making within the ecclesial and broader societal context, encouraging a stewardship of these traits when aligned with humility and service.

The melancholic temperament, depicted by black bile, is relatable to figures such as the Prophet Jeremiah, known for his introspection and pensive spiritual insights. Today, this temperament inspires an appreciation for deep reflective practices within the faith, advocating for a space where quiet contemplation and the pursuit of wisdom are esteemed as pathways to intimacy with the divine and personal transformation.

The phlegmatic, emblematic of phlegm, finds its modern interpretation as a peace-making and reliable force within the community. Such traits are requisite for harmonious societal and ecclesiastical coexistence, reflecting the biblical imperative for peace and reconciliation among the brethren, a notion ever so crucial in times marked by divisiveness and strife (Rouhiainen, 2020).

Modern psychology, while not explicitly employing the four humors, utilizes analogous categorizations to explore personality. For instance, the Big Five personality traits echo the four humors in their behavioral predictions and susceptibilities. In clinical applications, such constructs endorse introspection and self-knowledge, proving compatible with the biblical invitation to self-examination and alignment of one's character with Christ-like virtues.

Critics often argue that Hippocrates' humors are archaic and devoid of scientific grounding in the light of contemporary medical knowledge. Yet, their essence survives in the way we interpret personality dynamics by offering a heuristic device for comprehending human variance in temperaments. Their presence in academic circles, albeit less pronounced, is nonetheless palatable when considering personality's vast and unfathomable complexity in light of the imago Dei, the belief that humans are created in the image of God – a concept deeply rooted in Christian anthropology.

Though science marches on, and the humors have been largely discredited in medical practice, their illustrative power persists in psychological and spiritual counseling. The temperaments have frequently been woven into Christian teaching as a means to provide guidance on how individuals might navigate their predispositions in a way that honors both their creator and their own unique design.

Conclusively, while the four humors themselves are not explicitly referenced in the sacred scriptures, the corollary temperaments are alive and well in biblical hermeneutics. They inform the faithful's perceptions of sanctity, sin, and the pursuit of holiness. Integrating these historical perspectives with modern temperament theory opens avenues for rich dialogue between the teachings of the past and the discoveries of the present.

Thus, rather than diminishing the value of historical observation, contemporary psychology provides fresh semantics for age-old deductions. It confirms that the quest for understanding human nature is perpetual, transcending time, and embracing both reason and revelation. In this pursuit, the four humors stand as testament to humanity's enduring desire to know oneself – a task that remains as urgent today as it was under the azure skies of ancient Greece.

**The Jungian Personality Types and Biblical Archetypes**

The thorough exploration of personal and collective consciousness requires a marriage of psychology and theology, and nowhere is this more intriguing than in the Jungian theory of the psyche. We find within this framework a striking alignment with biblical archetypes, revealing a tapestry woven with threads of spiritual truth and psychological insight. The psyche, according to Carl Jung, is comprised of the ego, shadow, persona, and self (Jung, 1959); a holistic view that echoes the complexity of human characters found within the Scriptural narrative.

The ego represents the conscious mind in Jungian psychology, housing our sense of identity and agency. It's comparable to the biblical understanding of the 'heart' as the seat of personal agency and decision (Jeremiah 17:9). Yet, our hearts are often torn by conflict and contradiction, much like the ego's wrestle for control within the broader psyche.

The shadow is our unconscious aspect containing repressed weaknesses and desires, akin to the concept of 'sinful nature' expressed in Scripture (Romans 7:20). Biblical figures, such as David with his clandestine sin with Bathsheba, manifest a tangible shadow—an intrapsychic David battling the Goliath within.

Persona, the mask one wears in public life, resonates with St. Paul's exhortation to 'put on Christ' (Galatians 3:27)—not as a false front, but as a calling to incarnate virtue. This mirrors the transformation from persona (the masks of worldly expectation) to an authentic, Christ-like identity.

The Self, as the culmination and unity of the psyche, echoes the biblical call to become whole or holy (Matthew 5:48). In the Christian journey, this is found in the quest for sanctification—a unification of a person's inner life with the imago Dei in which they were created.

Biblical archetypes often reflect Jungian personality dimensions. Moses, for instance, represents the leader archetype—a complex mix of the Jungian functions of thinking and intuition, leading his people through a desert both real and metaphorical, in consistent engagement with his shadow while rooted firmly in his Self.

Similarly, Joseph's experience, from pit to pinnacle, reflects the Jungian individuation process (Genesis 37-41). His ego's maturation as a dreamer, his shadow during his enslavement, and his ultimate realization of his persona and True Self through tests of character and power—all resonate with the process of integrating and transcending these psychic elements.

Take the introverted prophet Elijah, retreating to the cave in a time of despair (1 Kings 19). His experience mirrors the inward journey of introversion, echoing Jung's belief in the necessity of embracing solitude to encounter the deeper aspects of the Self.

The New Testament character Peter, with his impetuous nature, illustrates the play between his ego and shadow through both grand confession and profound denial of Christ (Matthew 16:16, Matthew 26:74). His journey is a moving example of the Persona's failure, resulting in a transformative redemption that leads to a more unified Self.

Mary, the mother of Jesus, presents a unique Jungian archetype: the maiden whose ego is surrendered to divine purpose, whose shadow is scattered by the 'Magnificat' (Luke 1:46-55), and whose persona is a vessel for the incarnation of the Self—the Christ.

In these Jungian terms, the biblical narrative becomes rich with psychological meaning. Our identification with biblical figures serves not as just a spiritual exercise but as a profound modality for understanding the Self and our own journey toward individuation within the context of divine purpose.

It is critical to consider that while these parallels are striking, they're not an attempt to reduce biblical figures to mere psychological constructs. Rather, they are an effort to use the rigor of psychology to deepen our understanding of the spiritual dimensions of personality as revealed through holy narratives.

Addressing the Jungian shadow, for instance, is not solely a psychological imperative but resonates with the Christian mandate for repentance and self-reflection (Psalm 51). This process of reconciliation—of turning one's heart towards God—is both a psychological integration and a spiritual conversion.

Therefore, this chapter seeks to not only acquaint us with a more nuanced understanding of the Jungian theory but also to demonstrate how these psychological patterns find kinship with characters and themes in the biblical narrative, enriching our grasp of the human condition through the lens of revealed Truth.

The intertwining of Jung's psychological types with biblical archetypes serves as a striking reminder that the quest for understanding ourselves and our place within the cosmos has always been at the heart of both psychological inquiry and religious experience.

**The Psyche's Structure: Ego, Shadow, Persona, and Self**

In the vast landscape of the human psyche, the work of Carl Jung casts a long, scholarly shadow, illuminating the complex interplay of elements that comprise our inner world. One might conceive of the human psyche as a grand cathedral, with stained glass windows casting hues both vibrant and intricate. The structural components of this inner sanctum, as posited by Jung, are the Ego, Shadow, Persona, and Self. In deliberation upon their roles, one finds a fascinating synchrony with biblical typologies, an alignment that bolsters a Christian understanding of the soul's architecture.

The Ego, serving as the conscious mind, is the psychic structure that engages with daily reality and reason. It's the pilot in the vessel of the soul, charting the course through the seas of waking life. Yet, to regard the Ego in isolation is to overlook the profundity of its dependence on deeper, more enigmatic forces. As the scriptural adage urges us to self-examination, the Ego reflects the biblical injunction for self-awareness and moral accountability (James 4:8).

In the shadowy recesses of the psyche lies the Shadow, that repository of repressed desires and unacknowledged aspects of oneself. In the tradition of confession and repentance, Christianity recognizes the Shadow's existence, urging the faithful to confront and integrate these obscured facets of being (1 John 1:9). The process of acknowledging one's Shadow attests to an inherent pursuit of wholeness, mirroring the path of sanctification and the embrace of one's fallen nature.

Donning varied masks, the Persona represents the social facade, the part of the psyche oriented towards the external world. It is the aspect through which we relate to others and present an image that conforms to societal expectations. Comparably, the scriptures address the tensions between authenticity and outward appearances, entreating believers to commune with sincerity and truth (1 Samuel 16:7).

Amongst these diverse psychic elements, the Self stands as the integrating center, analogous to the divine order that beckons from the scriptural narrative. The Self is the archetype of wholeness, the culmination and reconciliation of all disparate parts (Colossians 1:17). This notion resonates with the biblical ethos of unity in the body of Christ, reflecting the spiritual journey towards integration and completeness in God.

It's important to note that Jung hypothesized the psyche as a dynamic system, where the Ego, Shadow, Persona, and Self are perpetually in dialogue, contending and commingling. The equilibrium of these interactions can be reflected in the Christian life, which is characterized by a constant struggle between virtue and vice, the call to repentance, and the transformative power of grace (Romans 7:15-25).

When digging deeper into the Shadow, we unearth aspects that Christian teaching mandates we must confront and subdue. The Shadow often contains elements antithetical to the virtues extolled in the Beatitudes, necessitating a process of transformation that echoes the concept of dying to oneself (Matthew 16:24).

The Persona, though useful in social navigation, becomes a source of spiritual tension when it conceals the truth of one's brokenness and fallen nature. The persona can be likened to the whitewashed tombs described by Christ—beautiful outwardly, yet inwardly filled with decay (Matthew 23:27).

The Ego's strategic position as the observer and decision-maker is akin to the biblical call for wise stewardship of one's life. It's through the Ego that one exercises free will, a gift granted by God but one that implicates individuals in the moral consequences of their actions (Deuteronomy 30:19).

As the Self strives for unity within the psyche, the Christian parallels this journey in the pursuit of theosis, or deification— the transformative process of becoming more like Christ. Just as the Self reconciles the conscious and unconscious realms, so does the believer seek oneness with God while navigating the complexities of human existence (2 Peter 1:4).

Individuals, in both psychological and spiritual development, experience a perpetual unveiling and refining of these components. Within the Christian context, these aspects of the psyche are not mere psychological constructs but are intimately tied to the soul's progression towards divine likeness.

In applying these Jungian concepts through the lens of Christian theology, a robust framework emerges, one that can address the aspects of the psyche without losing sight of their ultimate goal: the restoration of the imago Dei within the human being (Ephesians 4:24).

Jung's mapping of the psyche, while not explicitly religious, uncannily echoes the processes described in scripture: illuminate the hidden (Luke 12:2), present one's true self to God (Psalm 51:6), and pursue the unity and wholeness found in Christ (Ephesians 4:13). Being created in the image of a triune God, the desire for integration within the self and with the Creator mirrors the innate longing for relational unity and harmony that defines the Trinity itself.

The examination and integration of these psychic components compel devout reflection, penance, and transformation, aligning with the lifelong Christian journey towards sanctity. As such, the exploration of one's inner world through the structures identified by Jung becomes an act of obedience to the Christian calling, leading to greater self-awareness and spiritual maturity.

It is incumbent upon Christians to assimilate Jung's insights judiciously, ensuring that they serve to augment, rather than supplant, the foundational truths of their faith. Indeed, when woven with theological reverence, these structures offer a lens through which one may view the soul's intricate tapestry, enhancing both psychological integrity and spiritual growth.

**Biblical Figures and Corresponding Jungian Types** In the contemplation of biblical figures through the Jungian lens of psychological archetypes, we endeavour to uncover layers of the human psyche that mirror the multidimensional characters found within sacred scripture. Carl Jung's seminal work on personality types provides a framework where one can discern parallels between biblical narratives and psychological archetypes; here, we proceed to make such connections explicit.

Delving into the Jungian concept of the Self, we come to see figures such as Moses as embodiments of the archetypal ruler—commanding the Israelites with both authority and wisdom, akin to the extraverted thinking dominant type. His propensity to lead and establish laws is reflective of the Jungian desire for order and control within the collective unconscious (Jung, 1959).

In contrast, Abraham's journey of faith depicts the archetype of the explorer, aligning with the introverted intuition dominant type. Abraham's life was a pilgrimage in the truest sense, his destiny not foretold but revealed through introspective faith. It was not the material world that guided him but a profound sense of inner knowing—a hallmark of the introspective intuitive (von Franz, 1971).

King David presents as a potent mix of the artist and the warrior. His psalms exude the depth of the introverted feeling dominant type, pouring forth a raw and deeply personal spirituality. Yet, this internal world is balanced by David's extraverted sensing type evident in his acts of valor and impassioned leadership in battle (von Franz, 1971).

New Testament figures also resonate with Jungian constructs. For instance, the Apostle Paul stands out as the thinker, corresponding to the extraverted thinking dominant type. His epistles reveal a logical and systematic approach to theology and ethics, demonstrating a keen analytical mind engaged in the service of divine revelation (Jung, 1959).

Mary, the mother of Jesus, with her profound receptivity and contemplation, bears the markers of the introverted feeling dominant type. The internal, subjective valuation of experiences is paramount in her story, as seen in her pondering heart, which treasures and reflects on the divine mysteries (Jung, 1959).

The figure of Peter is emblematic of the sensation type. His initial impetuosity, the immediate response to Jesus's miracles, provides an illustrative study on the extraverted sensing dominant type. Peter's growth, however, into a pillar of the church reshapes him into a stabilizing force, displaying the developmental potential within each Jungian archetype (Jung, 1959).

Examining the duality of Judas Iscariot, we witness one of the darker archetypes, the shadow. Judas's complex character as both disciple and betrayer embodies the necessary interplay between light and darkness within the psyche. His betrayal, while provide a catalyst to salvation, also echoes the Jungian shadow's role in personal and collective transformation (Jung, 1959).

The story of Job invokes the archetype of the wise old man, correlating to the introverted intuition dominant type. Job's enduring patience amidst suffering, and his ultimate submission to the mystery of God's will, characterizes the deep, reflective wisdom associated with this type (von Franz, 1971).

The prophet Jeremiah exemplifies the archetype of the wounded healer. His personal afflictions and the resultant empathy for the suffering of his people align with the introverted feeling dominant type. Jeremiah's life embodies the Jungian understanding of how personal pain, when transformed, becomes a source of healing for others (Jung, 1959).

Solomon, in his quest for wisdom and subsequent authorship of Proverbs, embodies the Jungian teacher archetype, linked to the extraverted thinking dominant type. His search for understanding and the dissemination of that knowledge to his people reflects the archetype's desire for sharing enlightenment (von Franz, 1971).

Joseph, with his dream interpretation and foresight of Egypt's famine, acts within the contours of the visionary, an introverted intuition dominant type. His ability to perceive beyond the sensory world and to plan accordingly underlines the prophetic and intuitive faculties of this archetype (Jung, 1959).

The parable of the prodigal son can be reinterpreted through the lens of the Jungian hero archetype. The son's departure, subsequent degradation, and eventual redemption outline a hero's journey, a motif prevalent throughout Jung's archetypal studies—alluding to a kind of extraverted sensing that is initially misled but ultimately corrected (Jung, 1959).

Martha, sister of Lazarus, resonates with the extraverted sensing type associated with practical action and organization, an archetype often characterized by a penchant for tangible service and hospitality, as demonstrated through her attentive care of Jesus and her guests (Jung, 1959).

Finally, the figure of John the Baptist, with his ascetic lifestyle and clarion call for repentance, aligns with the Jungian sage, an introverted intuition dominant type. John's role as a spiritual herald and his introspective lifestyle underscore the archetype's characteristic drive for truth and enlightenment (von Franz, 1971).

In examining these diverse personalities, it is evident that the biblical narrative provides a rich tapestry from which to draw parallels with Jungian archetypes. This exploration fuses spirituality and psychology, offering a comprehensive vision of the human experience that embraces both the divinely inspired and the intrinsically human.

**Littauer's Personality Scheme: The Prophets and Apostles**

As we delve into Littauer's personality scheme, it is paramount to account for the rich tapestry of human dispositions manifested throughout biblical narratives. The essence of Littauer's model is to discern individual strengths and weaknesses, particularly within the contexts of ministry and witness. This discussion springs forth from prior explorations of personality through various lenses, now focusing specifically on the dynamic roles of the prophets and apostles.

The landscape of personality theory is akin to a fertile field, wherein Littauer's scheme emerges as a thoughtful cultivation of psychological insight, shaped by theological truths. Perhaps no other biblical figures exemplify Littauer's typology as vividly as the prophets and apostles, men driven by different forces, yet unified by a singular divine mission.

To understand Littauer's scheme in the setting of biblical narratives, consider the prophets, those divinely-inspired heralds who, in bearing the burdens of truth, demonstrated particular personality configurations. In the brazen resolve and fervor of Elijah, one may recognize the 'Choleric' temperament, inclined to leadership and decisiveness (Robins et al., 2007). Yet, amid his strengths, one also notes the tendencies toward impetuosity and an isolating doggedness.

Similarly, the apostles reveal the parameters of personality through their ministry. Take, for example, Peter, a man whose sanguine enthusiasm led him to walk on water, yet at times, the same impulsive spirit precipitated his shortcomings. Peter illustrates Littauer's teaching that personality comes coupled with both distinctive potential and predisposed limitations (Rosenman, 2019).

Littauer's typology does not confine itself to singular biblical moments but extends to the longitudinal paths these characters navigate. Paul, for instance, showcases another dimension of the 'Choleric' temperament. His transformation from Saul to Paul is a testament to the redeeming power that repurposes inherent drive and focus from destructive zeal to the passionate spread of the Gospel.

Contrastingly, the 'Melancholic' temperament resonates with the reflective and analytical minds of prophets like Jeremiah. His prophecies, steeped in sorrow and concern for adherence to God's law, expose the sensitivity and depth of the reflective individuals among us. This same temperament's potential for depression and paralysis by analysis reinforces that a temperament's gifts cannot be divorced from their associated trials (Ihsan& Furnham, 2018).

True comprehension of Littauer's personality scheme is furthered by examining the harmonic existence of qualities within the apostolic group. Thus, in James and John, the 'Sons of Thunder', who each mirrored 'Choleric' and 'Sanguine' temperaments, we discern the raw materials God refines through discipleship: ambition becomes godly assertiveness, and boisterousness transforms into vigorous advocacy for Christ's message.

Littauer's recognition of temperamental blends also invites us to consider the temperament of the 'Phlegmatic', perhaps seen in apostles such as Andrew, who quietly brought others to Christ. Phlegmatics offer stability and reliability at the risk of complacency, revealing how even the tranquil waters of a phlegmatic disposition can run deep with spiritual potential (Waisanen et al., 2015).

We are reminded that no personality scheme can fully enclose the imago Dei within each individual. Still, Littauer's model serves as an instructive framework, assisting us in perceiving the spectral diversity of the Apostles' characters—each honed for a unique yet complementary purpose in the tapestry of salvation history.

This perception links us back to a foundational Christian anthropology that emphasizes not only individuality but also community. The various Apostles, when considered collectively, represent a complete body in Christ, each member serving distinctively as purposed by our Creator.

Indeed, such a personality scheme should be understood as a tool, not a definitive map, that guides our contemplation of the human psyche. When we mirror the strengths and weaknesses depicted in the lives of the prophets and apostles, we realize that our personal dispositions, once submitted to God, can exceed mere temperament and serve a higher, divine narrative.

Therefore, when analyzing characters such as Moses, Elijah, Peter, or Paul, through Littauer's lens, we don't constrain these towering figures but instead appreciate the vibrancy with which God paints individual temperaments against a larger salvific backdrop. Moreover, this understanding aids us in pastoral care, teaching, and fellowship, as we continue to discern the workings of Providence through our own varied personalities.

In sum, the confluence of Littauer's typology with biblical narratives is not coincidental but an intricate part of how we comprehend God's workings through humanity's multifaceted nature. It reminds us that each person, each temperament, fits into a grand, celestial design—a design that respects personality diversity while fostering a unified mission in Christ.

As we move forward from this chapter, let us keep the essence of Littauer's wisdom, that personalities are both our instruments and our challenges, ever at the forefront. May we carry this understanding into every sphere of life, acknowledging that each individual encapsulates aspects of the prophets and apostles—each one called to transform their unique palette of temperaments into a lively portrait of faith in action.

### Identifying Personalities Through Biblical Narratives

Within the intricate weaving of biblical narratives, the distinct personas of prophets and apostles emerge as didactic exemplars, embodying the facets of personality that Littauer so eloquently categorizes. The exploration of such figures within scripture unveils a profundity of traits, motivations, and interpersonal dynamics, fostering an understanding of the divine infusion of character within the human experience. One comprehends profound dimensions of personality when the scripture is not merely read but lived, allowing the Word to penetrate the deepest recesses of one's psyche.

The prophet Elijah, with his fiery zeal and solitary bouts, may be characterized as one brimming with the choleric temperament. His resolve to challenge the prophets of Baal on Mount Carmel (1 Kings 18) demonstrates the audacity and decisiveness representative of such an individual. In contrast, the apostle John resonates with the sanguine, characterized by warmth and relational connectivity, mirrored in his designation as the 'disciple whom Jesus loved' (John 21:20-24) and his emphasis on love in his epistles.

Moses, an exemplary figure in scriptural narratives, epitomizes facets of the melancholic personality with his reflective and dutiful disposition. His meticulous attention to the directives of

Yahweh in tabernacle construction and his introspective encounter with God on Sinai (Exodus 25-31) underscore a temperament grounded in thoughtful deliberation and adherence to standards. Alternatively, the phlegmatic temperament finds a kindred spirit in the apostle Andrew, who calmly and consistently brought others to Christ, as illustrated by his introduction of the boy with the five loaves and two fishes (John 6:8-9).

These biblical exemplars serve as profound illustrations for present reflection. The embodiment of personality traits within the warp and woof of biblical narrative empowers the believer to grasp the continuity of the human saga, unified by the Creator's design. Each temperament, whether choleric, sanguine, melancholic, or phlegmatic, bears the imago Dei, providing glimpses into the multifaceted nature of humanity's relation to the divine.

Understanding the personalities of these scriptural figures also offers precious insight into the dynamics of ministry and witness. The manner in which Elijah confronted sin and indifference speaks to the vigor necessary for prophetic proclamation, while John's capacity for intimate fellowship hints at the relational essence of evangelism (McMinn, 2010).

Moreover, the interplay of these temperaments highlights the complementary nature of the body of Christ. Moses's lawgiving complements Aaron's priestly intercession, much like Paul's apostolic leadership was strengthened by Barnabas's encouragement (Acts 9:27). This emphasizes that the divine orchestration of personalities within the biblical context is not random; it's strategic and purposeful, calling for mutual edification within the Church.

The identification of these personalities through biblical narratives is not an anachronistic imposition of contemporary constructs upon ancient texts. Instead, it's an acknowledgment of the timeless and transcultural expressions of human temperament that are embedded within the fabric of sacred stories (Stack, 2000).

This implies a certain degree of universality in personality types that transcends eras and cultures. The heroes of faith embody traits that resonate with human experience across millennia, affirming the constancy of God's image imprinted upon humanity.

The narratives further serve as mirrors, reflecting back one's own dispositions and inclinations. In studying Elijah, one might discern a personal call to emboldened witness, or in contemplating John, recognize a need for deeper fellowship in one's walk with Christ. Thus, the biblical character becomes a lens for self-examination and spiritual formation.

In Paul's correspondence to the Ephesians, we discern a theological framework for understanding the mosaic of temperaments within the church (Ephesians 4:11-16). He articulates a vision for a community unified yet diverse, formed and functioning through the individualities God has bestowed upon each member. This insight points toward the necessity of each temperament's contribution to the full stature of Christ's body.

The study of prophets and apostles through the perspective of personality invites a richer appreciation of the virtue and vice inherent to each temperament. Elijah's boldness could slip into brashness, just as John's affability might risk compromising truth for the sake of peace. Scripture does not sanitize these figures; it reveals their complexity, offering the modern Christian a path to emulate their strengths and guard against their weaknesses (Stott, 1994).

The convergence of personalities and biblical narratives is pivotal in understanding not only human character but also the divine narrative itself. As humans engage with these stories, they are not merely acquainting themselves with ancient personalities but also with the living God who actively shapes and uses human temperament for His purposes.

Embarking on this exploration, one encounters the manifest Spirit who, through these narratives, illuminates the conscience, molds character, and invites each person to step into the grand story of redemption, armed with the understanding of their God-given temperament.

In a world yearning for identity and meaning, these scriptural exemplars offer a blueprint for recognizing and refining one's own personality through divine grace. The conscientious application of these insights into daily life stands at the heart of Christian discipleship and provides a testament to the enduring relevance of scripture in the pursuit of personal and communal holiness.

**Strengths and Weaknesses in Ministry and Witness** In scrutinizing the landscape of Littauer's personality scheme within the terrains of ministry and witness, one discerns a dual aspect inherent to each persona: strengths that serve as the bedrock for ministry, and weaknesses that, if not tempered, could undermine the very witness Christians are called to embody. This intricate interplay of qualities is illuminated in the light of the prophetic and apostolic examples, each diverse in their function, and yet quintessential to the body of Christ.

Consider the apostolic ministry: the fervent character of a Peter, or the analytical mind of a Paul. Each possessed strengths vital for the proliferation of early Christianity. Peter's boldness and Paul's intellect were harnessed in such a way as to give impetus to their respective ministries. Conversely, these same characteristics, were they not refined by grace, might have engendered weaknesses. Peter's impulsivity could have led him astray had it not been tamed by reflection (cf. John 21:15–19), and Paul's erudition could have edged into arrogance were it not for the "thorn in his flesh" that humbled him (2 Corinthians 12:7).

The strength of Littauer's scheme lies in its capacity to unravel these complexities. For the clerical soul or lay minister, self-awareness of one's natural proclivities is paramount. The strengths—be they leadership, empathy, intellect, or zeal—are gifts to be stewarded with humility. The weaknesses—propensity for power, excessive sensitivity, cognitive rigidity, or overzealousness—call for a vigilant self-scrutiny. It's a delicate balance that mirrors the interplay of faith and works, of divine grace and human effort.

How does this self-awareness translate into witness? An authentic witness is not merely one who professes faith, but embodies it. The minister's personal integration of strengths and weaknesses fortifies their credibility. In the public square, a ministry that is cognizant of its limitations is often more approachable, seen as authentic and thereby effective. Conversely, a ministry blind to its frailties may succumb to hypocrisy, which is the anathema of genuine witness and the caricature to which many a skeptic points.

Witness is as much about presence as it is proclamation. The strengths one brings into ministry—compassion, integrity, intuition—are the silent sermons that speak loudest. They are the tangible expressions of the Gospel's transformative power. Consequently, when one's weaknesses emerge—the irascible temper, the indecisiveness, the fear of man—these too must be offered up as homilies of human frailty, reminding the observant that grace is not yet perfected in us (Romans 7:15-19).

The Littauer scheme prompts ministers to embrace strengths not as personal accolades but as tools for serving others. Jesus exemplified this when he washed the disciples' feet, utilizing his authoritative strength in an act of profound humility (John 13:1-17). Similarly, recognizing one's weaknesses is a call to lean into the collective strength of the church, to find balance in the body's variegated gifts (1 Corinthians 12:12-27).

The integration of psychological insights with scriptural truths paves the way for a more nuanced approach to ministry. One that honors the complexity of the human condition, that sees man not as a monolithic entity but as a dynamic amalgam of saint and sinner, of divine image-bearer and fallible creature. This duality necessitates an ongoing conversion, a perpetual metanoia, that capacitates the minister to reflect an ever-clearer image of Christ to the world.

In practice, the ministry team must evaluate which strengths best align with various ministry tasks. A prophetic individual may thrive in preaching but may need support when it comes to pastoral care. Inversely, those with a gift for empathy might find themselves drained by the demands of administrative leadership without structured support.

One must not overlook the psychological stress that may stem from an imbalance of ministry responsibilities that play only to one's strengths while neglecting the cultivation of areas of weakness. The psychological literature on burnout and role stress underscores the importance of role diversification and the mitigation of role conflict to preserve the mental health and vitality of the minister (Simpkins, 1974).

In the context of witness, the discernment of strengths and weaknesses takes a public form. Ministry performed in self-awareness resonates authenticity; it is a witness to the transformative grace that takes men and women with all their foibles and fashions them into vessels of divine love (2 Corinthians 4:7).

Finally, self-awareness within ministry serves as a guardrail against the pitfalls of pride and despair. Knowledge of one's strengths can engender pride if not tempered by the remembrance that all good gifts come from above (James 1:17); awareness of one's weaknesses can lead to despair if not cushioned by the hope of God's power made perfect in our weakness (2 Corinthians 12:9).

The ministry, then, is a tapestry of divine grace woven with the threads of human personality. Each thread bears its unique hue, its strength, and weakness. When woven together under the guidance of the Divine Weaver, they form a tapestry that is both resilient and radiant, capable of withstanding the trials and tribulations of witness in a world that is at once broken and beautiful.

**Chapter 8: Myers-Briggs Type Indicator (MBTI) in the Light of Faith**

The Myers-Briggs Type Indicator (MBTI), a psychological assessment tool based on Carl Jung's theories, divides personalities into 16 distinct types, guided by four dichotomies: extraversion vs. introversion, sensing vs. intuition, thinking vs. feeling, and judging vs. perceiving (King, 1987). Yet, within the context of faith, particularly the Roman Catholic tradition, one must ponder how these categories align with the scriptural portrayal of human beings created imago Dei—in the image of God.

The dichotomy of extraversion and introversion captures the individual's propensity towards the external world or the internal self. This reflects the biblical call to both community engagement and solitary contemplation. Just as Christ withdrew to pray alone, He also ministered and taught among large crowds. The spiritual life often necessitates this balance, honoring both the outer work in the vineyard and the inner cultivation of the heart (Matthew 26:41).

Sensing and intuition delineate the means by which one perceives the world: through concrete, actual data or abstract, possible realities. The scriptures portray both the tangible evidence of God's work on Earth as well as the prophetic insight into His divine plans (Hebrews 11:1). Each has a place; the empirical Thomas needed to see and touch Christ's wounds (John 20:25-29), while John the Baptist, the prophet, heralded the coming of the Messiah through an intuitive recognition of the truth (Matthew 3:1-2).

Thinking and feeling contrast the preference for objective logic against subjective values in decision-making. Here, Paul's epistles demonstrate a logical explication of theology (Romans 12:1-2), whereas the Psalms pour forth emotional supplication and praise (Psalms 42:1-2), showing that faith engages both aspects of human discernment.

The final dichotomy between judging and perceiving speaks to the structure and spontaneity in one's life. The Bible extols both—the orderliness of creation (1 Corinthians 14:40) and the willingness to be moved by the Spirit (Galatians 5:25). Perceiving openness allows for divine interruptions, while judging structure affords stewardship and responsibility.

Integrating the cognitive functions as delineated by the MBTI with the virtues of faith illuminates their alignment to scriptural embodiment. The gifts of the Holy Spirit (1 Corinthians 12:4-11), such as wisdom, understanding, and counsel, resonate with the intuitive and thinking scales, while knowledge and piety reflect the sensing and feeling orientations.

Furthermore, the capacities inferred by the MBTI can assist in discerning vocation and spiritual gifts. Just as St. Paul writes of the body's many parts, each with a distinct function (1 Corinthians 12:12-27), so too does the MBTI suggest that differing personality types contribute uniquely to the ecclesial body. A keen understanding of one's type can serve as a guide in fostering God-given talents for the good of the Church.

Yet, there is a caution to be heeded. One's MBTI type should not become a box that confines or an excuse for complacency. The spiritual journey is one of transformation, and the Christian is called to the renewal of mind and spirit (Romans 12:2). The superficial adoption of MBTI descriptors must not overshadow the ineffable complexity of the human person, created in divine likeness.

It's crucial to acknowledge the criticisms as well. Some scholars debate the validity and reliability of the MBTI, citing psychological research that calls into question its empirical foundations (Ferreyra, 2007). Christians must approach such tools with discernment, balancing the insights they offer with the timeless truths of their faith.

Scriptural tradition offers rich narratives that complement psychological understanding. The MBTI's preference groupings can serve as a heuristic tool for exploring these biblical characters and their spiritual journeys. Acknowledging the dynamic nature of personality, the Catholic intellectual tradition invites engagement with psychological typologies while rooted in a worldview that transcends them.

Ultimately, the conjunction of the MBTI with Catholic thought should foster a both/and perspective. Faith and psychological insights need not be at odds but can instead inform each other, drawing individuals deeper into an understanding of the self that reflects both the gifts of creation and the hope of redemption.

The Church's history is decorated with saints and scholars who embodied diverse temperaments and charisms, illustrating the broad spectrum of God's creative genius. An appreciation for the variety of MBTI types within the communion of saints reveals the diversity of paths to holiness, each with its own form and coloration—yet all converging towards the same beatific vision.

In conclusion, the MBTI, when Illuminated by the light of faith, becomes more than a mere inventory of preferences; it transforms into a tool for self-discovery within the grand narrative of salvation history. As the faithful Christian navigates through the intricacies of personality, they are called to a higher integration, where individual traits harmonize within the symphony of God's redemptive work in the world.

**Cognitive Functions and Scriptural Embodiment**

In the intricate dance of psychology and spirituality, few systems of personality study stand as prominent as the Myers-Briggs Type Indicator (MBTI), a tool that categorizes individuals into sixteen distinct personality types based on a set of cognitive functions. These cognitive functions can be revered as mirrors, reflecting not only our psychological preferences but also, potentially, the divine imprint on our souls. To understand the harmonious relationship between MBTI and faith is to navigate through the vessel of our own cognitive abilities and scriptural embodiment.

At the heart of MBTI are the cognitive functions, which consist of sensing, intuition, thinking, and feeling, each further distinguished by their orientation as extraverted or introverted. This dualistic nature of the cognitive functions resonates with the Pauline conception of the flesh and the spirit; where one is oriented toward the external world, the other looks within, seeking a more profound truth. We can discern a scriptural parallel in Romans 7:22-23, which speaks of the inner conflict between the laws of God and the laws of sin.

Extraverted sensing (Se) and introverted sensing (Si), as perceptual functions, denote our capacity to engage with the present and the past. Far from being merely psychological constructs, these functions echo the biblical emphasis on mindfulness and remembrance. As faithful stewards of our senses, we are called to embody the teachings of Christ, ever-mindful of the lilies of the field (Matthew 6:28-30) and the manna from heaven (Exodus 16), mindful that God provides and teaches in the here and now.

Intuition, both extraverted (Ne) and introverted (Ni), serves as the conduit for insight and foresight, encouraging us to look beyond the immediate to the abstract and eternal. Akin to the scriptural call for wisdom (Proverbs 4:7), intuition prompts us to seek a divine perspective, to discern not just with the eyes, but with the heart. It's in the scriptural embodiment of Joseph's interpretation of dreams (Genesis 40) where we see the validation of forethought blessed by God's own revelatory purpose.

Thinking, whether extraverted (Te) or introverted (Ti), can indeed be understood as the logical facet of our nature, reminiscent of the biblical appeals for discernment and righteousness in judgment. It encourages the pursuit of a methodical understanding, as seen in the measured wisdom of Solomon (1 Kings 3:16-28). Yet, in the face of such analytical prowess, the scriptural call remains – not to lean solely on one's understanding but to trust in the Lord with one's whole heart (Proverbs 3:5-6).

Feeling, both extraverted (Fe) and introverted (Fi), reflects our evaluative criteria of worth, closely resonating with the scriptural exhortations to love, compassion, and empathy. As Paul conveyed to the Corinthians, if we have not love, we are nothing (1 Corinthians 13:2). It is this cognitive function that beckons us to embody the scriptural virtue of charity – to clothe ourselves in heartfelt kindness, humility, and patience (Colossians 3:12).

When examined through a lens of faith, each cognitive function can be seen not only as a psychological instrument but also as an essential component of spiritual living. The embodiment of these functions reveals the depth of their scriptural significance. Like facets of a gem crafted by the Creator, they reflect the Light in unique ways, guiding us towards holistic living that integrates both mind and soul.

To be sure, the MBTI itself must not become an idol, but it may serve as a map leading to an understanding of how our unique cognitive dispositions align with our calling. May it never be forgotten that each function has its place within the body of Christ, contributing to the edification of the whole, much as individual parts contribute to the fullness of the body (1 Corinthians 12:12-27). Thus, we discern that there is a divine purpose in each cognitive preference, guiding us in our ministry and our witness.

The Introverted Intuition of one person may unfold the eschatological truths hidden within the symbols of Revelation, while the Extraverted Sensing of another may manifest Christ's presence through practical acts of service. It's in the diversity of these functions, much like the diversity of spiritual gifts (Romans 12:4-8), that the body of believers finds its strength.

It's worth considering how even Christ Himself exemplified the balance of cognitive functions. He engaged His senses fully in the present moment, yet He also saw beyond the temporal with perfect intuition. He displayed impeccable logical judgment while simultaneously operating from a core of unconditional love and compassion.

In applying these insights, it's crucial to approach the MBTI with humility and discernment. Our understanding of ourselves, informed by the cognitive functions, must be submitted to a greater understanding – that of God's sovereignty and design. The goal is not merely self-knowledge, but self-transformation in the light of divine truth, as we conform to the image of the Son (Romans 8:29).

Therefore, the scriptural embodiment of cognitive functions within the MBTI model stands as an opportunity for profound integration, inviting us to explore the dimensions of our own heart and mind in communion with the Word. Engaging in scriptural embodiment is to recognize that while the cognitive functions provide a framework, it is the spirit that gives life (2 Corinthians 3:6).

Scriptural understanding of the person augments our grasp of the cognitive functions, providing us with a more fulfilled vision of human anthropology as it intersects with personal development. It's here where the cognitive models of psychology meet the redemptive narrative of faith. Thus, scriptural embodiment transcends the secular interpretation of MBTI, transforming it into a tool for spiritual edification and self-reflection.

In conclusion, it's essential to acknowledge that while the cognitive functions of MBTI present a robust framework for understanding personality, their fullest expression is realized within the context of a faith that embraces the whole person—body, mind, and spirit—and looks to the Creator for ultimate meaning and purpose. It is here, at the crossroads of cognitive science and divinely revealed truth, that we find a path forward, a way to live out our faith through the very cognitive faculties we have been endowed with.

**Discerning Vocation and Spiritual Gifts via MBTI**

The contemplation of one's vocation and the discernment of spiritual gifts are integral to the Christian pilgrimage. This journey is illuminated by the light of the Myers-Briggs Type Indicator (MBTI), a tool that categorizes individuals into psychological types. By examining the propensities brought forth by their MBTI type, one can gain profound insights into how God may be calling them to serve within His grand narrative (Jung, 1921).

As believers are called according to their unique design, the MBTI offers a prism through which the kaleidoscopic variety of their aptitudes are viewed. Diving into this study, one can't help but wonder how, for instance, an ENFP might be naturally poised to evangelize with an infectious joy, or how an ISTJ could exemplify a steadfast commitment to service and order within the church (Inman, 2023).

The peculiar beauty of the Christian doctrine lies in its affirmation that each person is endowed with gifts meant to fortify the body of Christ. In this vein, the MBTI does not clash with the ecclesiastical understanding but rather can enhance it by providing a framework to recognize these gifts in oneself and others (Romans 12:4–8).

The task of discerning one's vocation requires a deep-rooted knowledge of self, which is where MBTI steps in as a facilitator. For example, those who identify as INFJs often report feeling a pull towards vocations that involve counseling and guiding, reflecting perhaps the spiritual gift of prophesy in the Pauline sense – the ability to speak truths that build up the congregation (1 Corinthians 14:3).

Similarly, individuals exhibiting preferences for INTJ may find themselves naturally inclined towards discerning complex theological and philosophical concepts, potentially echoing the gift of wisdom. This inclination can lead them towards intellectual vocations that serve the Church's magisterial role in teaching (James 3:17).

One cannot contemplate MBTI through the faith lens without considering the notion of free will intrinsic to the Christian worldview. While MBTI may outline predispositions, it is ultimately the individual's choice to cultivate their spiritual gifts and respond to God's call, which aligns with the personalistic psychology that respects the agency of the person (Greggo, 2011).

In the sacramental life of the church, MBTI can serve as an aid to vocational discernment. An ESFP, known for their spontaneity and fervor, might be called to liturgical worship ministries, finding in the dynamic expressions of praise a kindred channel for their energy, thereby enriching the communal worship experience.

Within the contemplative tradition, the integration of MBTI in spiritual direction can assist individuals in navigating their interior life. An ISTP might struggle with conventional prayer forms yet find solace and connection with God in ignition spirituality, which can be tailored to their concrete, problem-solving oriented nature.

This potential of MBTI to harmonize with the pursuit of faith and service is not without its detractors. Some may argue that pigeonholing individuals into types runs the risk of overlooking the imago Dei in each person, reducing the mystery of the human soul to a mere set of characteristics (Brooten, 1996). It's crucial, therefore, to leverage MBTI as a starting point rather than a definitive conclusion on one's capabilities and calling.

Take the ESTJ type, often associated with management and leadership. In a church setting, this could translate to a natural capacity for church administration or leadership roles within ministry. Beyond mere organizational skills, this may be a manifestation of the biblical gift of administration, the often overlooked but critical aspect of sustaining the practical aspects of church life (1 Corinthians 12:28).

Using MBTI to discern one's spiritual gifts should go hand in hand with prayer, counsel from the faith community, and an openness to the Holy Spirit's guidance. It's not a tool that replaces spiritual discernment but rather complements it by offering tangible pathways for one's inclinations and energies to be channeled towards God's service.

As this discussion integrates MBTI into the fabric of discerning vocation and spiritual gifts, it highlights the need for careful and prayerful interpretation of these psychological insights. They should inform but never limit the understanding of how God can work uniquely and mysteriously in each individual's life (1 Corinthians 12:6).

In summary, MBTI holds the promise of playing a constructive role in discerning vocation and spiritual gifts. It's an instrument, akin to many others at the service of faith, capable of guiding individuals towards understanding their role in the Church's mission. Moreover, it can enhance one's commitment to finding where the natural inclinations of temperament can meet God's divine calling (Romans 8:28).

It becomes imperative, then, to adopt a balanced view of MBTI within the broader context of faith, recognizing that the indicator is not a divine oracle but a psychological compass that can help steer believers in the right direction when used judiciously and in harmony with divine revelation.

**Chapter 9: Kiersey Temperament Sorter and the Disciples of Christ**

In the deliberation of temperament and its implications on the Christian community, one must consider the synthesis of psychological insight with theological tradition. The Keirsey Temperament Sorter emerges as a tool resonant with the enduring narrative of the Gospels, particularly when pondered alongside the diverse ensemble of Christ's disciples. It categorizes individuals into four primary temperaments: Guardian, Artisan, Idealist, and Rational, each with its distinctive characteristics.

Guardians are often seen as stabilizing forces within a group—practical, systematic, and reliable—mirroring the steadfastness of disciples like Andrew, who was foundational in building the early Church. Artisans, with their adaptable, skillful, and audacious natures, could be likened to the zeal of Peter, ever the impetuous fisherman willing to venture into unknown waters.

The Idealists, with their authentic, empathetic, and benevolent inclinations, reflect the heart of John, the disciple whom Jesus loved, with his profound capacity for love and relationship. The Rational temperaments, analytical, strategic, and curious, resonate with the thoughtful skepticism and eventual steadfast belief of Thomas, ever the inquisitive inquirer after truth.

In assessing the disciples through the lens of Keirsey, one must not oversimplify their personas or constrain them within the strict bounds of modern temperament theory. Still, it is fruitful to examine how their varied personalities coalesced into a dynamic force for the early church.

The practical utility of the Keirsey Temperament Sorter in contemporary Christian communities lies in its ability to foster understanding and encouragement of individuality within a collective unity. Through recognizing the innate dispositions each member brings to the Body of Christ, better appreciation of each one's unique contribution to the church's mission can be realized.

More importantly, one must scrutinize these personality distinctions within the divine paradigm of sanctification: for the temperament, though unique, is yet subject to the transformative power of grace. The Rational can learn trust beyond analysis; the Guardian can embrace faith that defies structure; the Artisan can submit their spontaneity to divine inspiration; and the Idealist can temper their idealism with the wisdom of reality in Christ.

In relation to evangelization work, temperamental awareness equips members of the Christian community to align their approaches with the intrinsic capacities that God bestowed upon them. The Apostle Paul exhorts believers to consider their gifts in doing God's work (Romans 12:6-8), implying a customized strategy in fulfilling the Great Commission.

Furthermore, as each temperament group is predisposed to communicate and perceive the world distinctly, the Gospel message must be manifold in its expression to effectively resonate with diverse audiences. Hence, the Apostle's missions can be seen as tailored to their inherent strengths, demonstrating how divine providence orchestrates a harmonious symphony from a variety of individual notes.

The perceptiveness of the Keirsey Temperament Sorter's stratifications is not, however, an end in itself but rather a means through which one can approach service within the church. A Guardian's administrative efficacy, an Artisan's imaginative ministry, an Idealist's inspirational visions, and a Rational's critical tenets become indispensable within the Christian fabric when applied sagaciously.

Within the cooperation of these configurations of the human psyche, there is an echo of the trinitarian existence - unity in distinction. While acknowledging the enduring uniqueness of individual temperaments, there is a devotion to a collective identity in Christ which must supersede all.

The intrinsic value in understanding oneself and others through temperamental analysis is ultimately grounded in the pursuit of a more harmonious Christian relationship. The acceptance and embodiment of one's distinctive temperament can facilitate a more profound engagement with spiritual disciplines, leading to a more authentic expression of faith and community life.

In conclusion, the reflection of temperaments among the disciples and their respective roles in the apostolic mission serves as an invitation to ruminate on the evidence of a creative Creator. One who designs diversity not as an obstacle but as an asset to the communal and divine quest for salvation.

What then shall be said of the Kiersey Temperament Sorter in the context of a faith-seeking understanding? Let it be recognized as a beneficial instrument, primarily when used to highlight variations within the ecclesial body, magnifying thereby the Facilitator of diversity - the very Author of life.

As disciples today conform to the likeness of Christ, they must recognize the formulation of temperament as a dynamic interplay between the Creator's design and the redemptive work through Christ, affirmed by the continuous guidance of the Holy Spirit.

**Matching Apostolic Missions to Temperament Groups**

In the annals of the Christian tradition, the disciples of Christ operate not merely as historical figures but as embodiers of divine telos, having traversed the intrinsic expanses of human temperament to fulfill heavenly missions. The Keirsey Temperament Sorter, a contemporary cognition of Jungian typology, serves as an instrumental lens through the prism of which we may discern how apostolic missions align with temperament groups. This task we attempt, mindful of the sovereignty of Providence over the congenital dispositions of these pivotal men.

The Guardian temperament, exemplifying dependability and service, echoes in the steadfast presence of James the son of Alphaeus. His relative obscurity in scripture crafts a paradigm of the unheralded faithful, often the backbone of ecclesial communities, serving without fanfare or earthly reward. As the guardians in our midst uphold traditions and maintain the bedrock of societal structures, so too did such individuals prop the fledgling communities of early Christendom (Sweet, 2009).

The Idealist quadrant of temperaments, characterized by their desire for meaning and integrity in interpersonal relations, finds a counterpart in John the Evangelist. With a heart aflame with divine love and a vision towards the transcendent, John conveyed a theology deeply rooted in the interconnectivity of the Godhead and humanity. In contemporary terms, Idealists aspire to harmonize their inner convictions with outer actions, much like John, who intertwined the necessity of love within the fabric of Christian praxis (Miller, 2001).

The Rational temperament, pursuant of knowledge and competence, can be matched to the apostle Thomas, with his well-documented quest for understanding. Thomistic inquiries should not be confused with a deficit of faith; rather, they are indicative of a zeal for truth that refuses to settle for the superficial. It is the Rational's contribution to the Christian mission to quarry deeper into the bedrock of faith, to question, and by questioning, to understand more profoundly the veracity of the Incarnation (Bos, 2021).

Lastly, the Artisan temperament displays adaptability and a proclivity for pragmatic action, mirrored in the demeanor of Peter, the impetuous fisherman who evolved into the 'Rock'. His leadership was not without flaw, for what human exemplar is unmarred, yet his practicality and responsiveness to the promptings of the Holy Spirit were the forge upon which the early Church was hammered into shape.

When contemporary Christians reflect upon the Apostles through the Keirsey Temperament Sorter, a tapestry of divine wisdom emerges in the allocation of temperaments. These allocations—Providence's own doing—are seen not as arbitrary but as instrumental in the advancement of the Gospel.

It is then clear that a correlation exists between the temperament of the apostles and the unique nature of their respective missions. The fusion of psychological understanding and divine purpose in the work of the Apostles provides an exemplar for bringing the unique gifts of each temperament to bear in the life of the Church today (Malphurs, 2006).

In this endeavor, the modern believer is afforded the opportunity to consider their temperament not as a fixed caveat upon their spirit, but as an invitation from the divine to participate in a grand apostolic mission. Each temperament group offers strengths to be acknowledged, and areas of growth to be approached with humility and grace.

As each apostle has showcased, there is no temperament devoid of a role within the Body of Christ. The Guardian offers steadfastness, the Idealist illuminates with vision, the Rational emboldens with inquiry, and the Artisan advocates through dexterity. Collectively, they create a mosaic reflective of the divine intention for human diversity within unity.

It becomes incumbent upon the Church to not merely catalog temperament but to harness it towards the ecclesial mission.

Through understanding, we can allocate roles within the community that optimize each member's inherent capabilities and dispositions, thereby enhancing both individual fulfillment and collective efficacy.

The congruency of the Keirsey Temperament Sorter with the needs of the early Christian community serves as a testament to the transcendent utility of temperament understanding. Just as the early disciples were shepherded by Christ to overcome innate proclivities and assume their apostolic roles, so too are Christians today called to a similar transformation—cultivating their temperamental inclinations not as ends in themselves, but as means to a higher, communal purpose.

One can't help but ponder if the disciples themselves were aware of their temperamental strengths and weaknesses, and how these contributed to the broader mission of the early Church. This reflection beckons the faithful to consider their own roles in the world today, and how their temperaments may guide their paths in the pursuit of vocation and spiritual growth (Larrimore, 2001).

It is in this vein that the Keirsey Temperament Sorter becomes not only a tool for self-understanding but for divine collaboration. The correlation between apostolic missions and temperament groups serves as an enduring demonstration that, in the grand narrative of redemption, every penchant and proclivity has been foreseen and factored into the providential blueprint of salvation history.

Consequently, the discipline of psychology, when rightly ordered and integrated into the realm of faith, paves the way toward sanctification. It invites a profound introspection which harmonizes who we are, our most intrinsic traits, with the mission to which we are called in Christ—a mission that, in the fullness of time, will culminate in the eschatological triumph of the Church, the Bride of the Lamb.

**Individuality and Unity in the Christian Community**

In considering the Kiersey Temperament Sorter within the context of the Disciples of Christ, we embark upon a delicate balance between the individual nature of faith and the communal expression thereof. As the Christian community is comprised of diverse individuals, each bestowed with unique gifts and temperaments, there emerges a rich tapestry portraying the manifold wisdom of God (Ephesians 3:10). The apostolic missions, as outlined in the scriptures, present a profound reflection of this diversity harmonized within the unity of the church.

The individuality inherent in the members of the Christian community is not simply an accident of creation but a purposeful design, which mirrors the complexity and individuality found within the Triune God Himself. Just as the Father, Son, and Holy Spirit exhibit distinct personal characteristics within a perfect unity, so too is the church called to reflect a multitude of temperaments working in concert (1 Corinthians 12:12-14).

This unity, frequently expounded upon by the Apostle Paul, does not imply uniformity; rather, it is a symphony of differentiated parts. The Kiersey Temperament Sorter, which categorizes individuals into distinct personality types, is not to segregate but to celebrate differing inclinations, each contributing distinctly to the edification of the Body of Christ (Romans 12:4-5).

Consider the diversity amongst Christ's own disciples. Peter's choleric leadership contrasts with John's more phlegmatic, loving disposition, exemplifying how different temperaments fulfill various roles within the gospel narrative. Kiersey's tool can help illuminate how such differing personas can coalesce into a single, effective ministry without compromising the individual character granted by the Creator (Strong, 2017).

The integrity of personal identity within the fabric of community takes on a metaphorical semblance to the incarnation: Christ, fully God yet fully man, embodies both the divine and the human. In individual believers, the uniqueness of one's temperament is sanctified by God's presence, capable of freely exhibiting His graces while maintaining its character (Colossians 3:10).

Furthermore, the Christian community, instructed to bear one another's burdens (Galatians 6:2), can become a space where the interdependence of individual temperaments is made evident. Kiersey's framework provides a structured understanding of how these temperaments may interplay, necessitating a communal environment where such burdens may be shared and carried collectively.

In practice, the appreciating of individual temperaments within Christian fellowship can enhance the ministry's effectiveness. Those of a more practical, sensing temperament serve the church through tangible acts of service, while those endowed with intuitive and perceiving traits contribute through visionary leadership and prophetic insight. Thus, each temperament becomes a unique blessing and resource to the community of believers (Corinthians 12:7).

The very act of communion, a sacramental manifestation of unity, serves as an emblem of diversity unified under the headship of Christ. The bread, symbolizing the body, is composed of many grains, and the wine, the blood, is pooled from many grapes. Similarly, Kiersey's interpretation of individual temperaments when consecrated to God depicts not a divisive scheme but a hallowed and integrative approach reflecting the beauty of diversity within unity (1 Corinthians 10:17).

The practice of discernment is enhanced through our understanding of individual temperaments. Within the Christian community, acknowledging and employing temperament insights can support the identification of one's calling, be it lay ministry, monastic life, or any other vocation to which a believer might aspire. It is the unique traits that enable the individual to resonate with their God-given purpose (Romans 12:6).

Critics may argue that categorization risks pigeonholing individuals, potentially stifling the Spirit's spontaneity. However, within a robust Christian framework, temperaments serve as a starting point for growth and development, not a deterministic confinement. As the Spirit gifts individuals differently, it is these temperaments refined through spiritual maturity and virtue that propel the believer forward (Galatians 5:22-23).

Furthermore, embracing the heterogeneity of temperaments within the church context acts as a living testimony to the world of God's creative plurality. In a culture often insistent on uniformity and conformity, the Christian community, through its understanding and application of temperament insights, stands as a counter-cultural beacon of God's expansive love (John 13:35).

The Kiersey Temperament Sorter, seen through the lens of faith, does not objectify the individual but rather sanctifies one's psychological structure for the sake of community. In doing so, the Christian community becomes a reflection of the holy city, a Jerusalem composed of every tribe, tongue, and nation, each individual glorifying God in a distinct but harmonious voice (Revelation 7:9).

For the Christian community, understanding temperaments is thus a means of honoring the imago Dei within each person, affirming their intrinsic value while encouraging harmonious relations within the body of Christ. The Scriptures teach that there is variety in God's gifts but the same Spirit, diversity in service but the same Lord, and manifold workings but it is the same God who inspires them all in everyone (1 Corinthians 12:4-6).

To conclude, the integration of the Kiersey Temperament Sorter into the Christian community's discourse assists in elucidating the mystery of individuality and unity as coexistent realities. This truth, deeply embedded in the gospel, invites believers to fully embrace their personal temperaments while actively participating in the communal life of faith, thus advancing the Kingdom in its splendid diversity and unity.

## Chapter 10: DISC Assessment and Biblical Leadership Styles

The DISC assessment tool stands as a monument in the psychological landscape, measuring four primary behavioral traits: Dominance, Influence, Steadiness, and Compliance. It is the embodiment of an understanding that human behavior is not arbitrary but flows from distinctive, measurable patterns. As we delve into the DISC assessment, we do so with a conviction that such patterns are not products of a secular construct alone but are observable in the divinely inspired text of the Bible, offering a profound framework for biblical leadership styles.

Consider the Dominance trait – the drive to exert influence over events and people. In biblical narratives, leaders with high dominance moved with authority and decisiveness. Moses stood before Pharaoh, unyielding in his demand for the release of his people (Exodus 5:1-2). His leadership under God's command exemplified dominance characterized by a righteous pursuit. This blending of psychological understanding with theological insight directs us to acknowledge a correspondence between human behavior and divine ordination.

Influence, characterized by the ability to persuade and inspire others, is vividly manifested in the ministry of the Apostle Paul. The text of his Epistles demonstrates a persuasive power anchored not in manipulation but in a deep conviction of the

Gospel's truth. Paul's leadership approach aligns with those in the DISC framework who exhibit high influence, confirming that ancient wisdom pertains to and is reflected in contemporary evaluative metrics (2 Corinthians 5:11).

Steadiness is another DISC factor, seen in consistent and cooperative behaviors that foster a stable environment. The patience of Job, despite his sufferings, embodies a profound steadiness (Job 1:20-22). His ability to remain steadfast under trial reflects the advantages of such a trait in any epoch and under any circumstance, uniting the insights of the DISC assessment with the virtuous example set forth in scripture.

The final DISC trait, Compliance, refers to the propensity for structured and rule-abiding behavior. Daniel, whose adherence to dietary laws demonstrated not only personal conviction but also a commitment to divine standards, exemplifies high compliance (Daniel 1:8-16). His actions mirror the principle that celebration of order and respect for authority serve as foundational elements of both societal and spiritual wisdom.

These four quadrants of the DISC model each find their echo in the scriptures, suggesting that contemporary psychology, though secular in many of its tenets, resonates with the ancient wisdom preserved in biblical literature. It brings to light that human behaviors and predilections are not merely random but participate in a larger, providentially ordered tapestry.

Discussing leadership styles with the DISC model provides articulate frameworks to decipher human conduct whilst remaining mindful of the divine presence in shaping human history. Modern-day leaders within the Church can find parallels between their DISC profiles and those of biblical figures, hence integrating both contemporary understandings of leadership with those etched into the perennial narratives of scripture.

Moreover, this convergence of psychological models with scriptural exegesis may yield a richer discernment process. One which not only acknowledges the individual's propensities but also how these characteristics may be aligned with the divine will as demonstrated by biblical exemplars.

The application of the DISC assessment to biblical leadership styles is not an exercise in proof-texting or attempting to retrofit modern psychology into ancient texts. Rather, it is a recognition that human nature possesses enduring traits, which, when viewed through the lens of faith, take on a deeper resonance.

Beneath the surface, ease of reconciliation between the DISC model and biblical figures suggests a more profound, perhaps ontological, congruence between the structures of the human psyche and the life of faith. Such an alignment intimates that virtues extolled by scripture are not arbitrary but correspond to an innate order within humanity.

It should be noted that while these correlations exist, caution is due when imbuing psychological models with a level of authority equivalent to sacred scripture. Psychometrics, including DISC, are tools aiding in self-awareness and leadership development, and they should be engaged with in a manner befitting their status as human constructs. Their utility in comprehending behavior patterns must therefore remain subservient to the revealed truth of Holy Writ.

In contemplating the DISC model and its correspondence to biblical leadership, we touch upon the essential unity of truth – be it derived from systematic observation or divine revelation. For the Church, the assessment of leadership styles through the DISC framework provides a contemporary language to talk about personal and ministerial qualities which, though articulated with modern terminology, are timeless in their essence.

Finally, the integration of the DISC model into our understanding of biblical leadership does more than offer parallels; it communicates the notion that every trait, every inclination of the human person, can be guided toward God's purposes. Whether one is dominant or steady, influential or compliant, each style of leadership finds appropriateness in service to God's kingdom.

In conclusion, as we merge the wisdom of DISC with the insights of scripture, we furnish the faithful with tools to more accurately discern their gifts and roles within the Body of Christ. This endeavor supports believers in their quest to holistically integrate their faith with every facet of their human experience, advancing the Church's mission in the modern age.

## Dominance, Influence, Steadiness, and Compliance in Biblical Figures

The DISC assessment, a system for categorizing personality traits, offers a framework for analyzing human behavior in various contexts, including the rich tapestry of Biblical narratives. This section aims to delve into the correspondence between the DISC dimensions—Dominance (D), Influence (I), Steadiness (S), and Compliance (C)—and the personas of select biblical figures, offering readers a thoughtful integration of psychological insight with theological reflection.

Dominance, the trait characterized by assertiveness and control, is manifested in the Biblical figure of Moses. Moses, as a leader of the Israelites, displayed a decisive and determined will to lead his people out of Egyptian bondage (Exodus 3:10). His resolve in confronting Pharaoh and his initiative in leading the Israelites through the desert demonstrate the D characteristic of taking command in challenging situations (Campbell, 2007).

Similarly, King David epitomizes a blend of Dominance and Influence. While demonstrating the assertiveness of a warrior and a king, David also exhibited a charismatic presence that won the hearts of the Israelite nation (1 Samuel 18:6-7). His ability to inspire through psalms and leadership illustrates the magnetic appeal that characterizes the I dimension of the DISC model (Rushmore).

Influence is further seen in the Apostle Paul, whose epistles reflect a persuasive and sociable nature, an integral aspect of the I personality. Paul's letters were instrumental in encouraging and growing the early church, displaying a profound understanding of relational dynamics and an ability to communicate effectively across diverse cultures (Romans 1:11-12; Keller, 2004).

Steadiness, characterized by loyalty and consistency, is evident in the life of Abraham. Abraham's unwavering faith in God's promises, despite uncertain and prolonged circumstances, exemplifies behavioral steadiness. His patient journey, culminating in the birth of Isaac, captures the essence of the S trait, defined by a stable and methodical approach to life's trials (Hebrews 11:8-12).

The figure of Ruth also showcases steadfastness, as her steadfast loyalty to Naomi and adherence to the God of Israel illustrate the serene and cooperative nature of the S trait. Despite personal loss and cultural displacement, Ruth's narrative underscores her steady devotion and reliable support (Ruth 1:16-17).

Compliance, the trait marked by attention to standards and accuracy, is portrayed in the person of the prophet Daniel.

Daniel's careful adherence to dietary laws, even in the foreign court of Babylon, and his meticulous interpretation of dreams and visions exemplify the qualities of compliance and analytical thinking (Daniel 1:8; Daniel 5:12).

The disciple Thomas, often labeled "Doubting Thomas," presents a nuanced view of the compliance trait. His request for empirical evidence of Christ's resurrection aligns with the analytical and skeptical aspects of the C personality, which seeks confirmation and clarity before commitment (John 20:24-29).

Understanding these biblical figures through the DISC framework not only illuminates the diversity of personalities within Scripture but also showcases how various traits are harnessed for God's purposes. It emphasizes that each personality type, when guided by divine wisdom, can contribute uniquely to the unfolding story of salvation (1 Corinthians 12:4-6).

These exemplars challenge the faithful to perceive character traits not merely as psychological constructs, but as elements designed by God, the Creator, for the flourishing of individuals within the tapestry of His redemptive plan. Personalities are not static but are dynamic interfaces between the Creator's intention and human free will.

It is worth noting that the personality styles delineated by the DISC assessment are neutral in themselves; it is the orientation and application of these traits that can lead to virtuous or sinful behavior. The Bible exemplifies how dominance may equate to protective leadership in Moses or tyrannical rule in Pharaoh; influence can engender empowering encouragement as seen in Paul or deceitful manipulation as found in Jezebel (1 Kings 21).

Similarly, steadiness grants Abraham the perseverance to inherit the promise, whereas in other figures, it may produce complacency and inaction. Compliance undergirds Daniel's prophetic insight but can also lead to legalism and an obsession with the letter of the law over its spirit, as seen in Pharisaical practices (Mark 7:1-13).

This integration summons one to behold the myriad ways God uses personalities within His redemptive arc and invites the consideration of how our own temperaments can align with divine purpose. It is through the transformation of our characters by the Holy Spirit that personality becomes a conduit of God's grace, contributing to the growth and edification of the body of Christ (2 Corinthians 3:18).

Given this rich interplay between character and destiny, the study of biblical figures through the lens of DISC aids in discerning lessons for contemporary leadership within the church. Followers of Christ are called to consider how elements of dominance can be directed towards godly stewardship, how influence can be used to positively shape community, how steadiness can be applied to faithfully endure in trials, and how compliance can lead to a higher standard of holiness and truth.

In conclusion, the DISC model presents a useful, though not exhaustive, framework for interpreting biblical personalities. It aligns with the overarching Christian anthropology that views human traits as reflective of the imago Dei--the image of God--which is both the source and summit of all Christian virtue. The discourse on personality within the context of divine revelation inspires a deeper contemplative outlook that transcends mere scholarly analysis or clinical categorization.

**Drawing Parallels with Ancient Wisdom and Modern
Practice**

In ancient times, introspection and understanding of the self
were disciplines as venerated as they were mysterious, often
entwined with philosophical and theological considerations of
human nature. While modern psychology offers us the DISC
assessment - a tool for detailing human behavior across four
categories - we find semblances of these insights echoed in
scriptural narratives.

The biblical depiction of leaders and prophets often showcases
traits that we now comprehend through the lenses of
Dominance, Influence, Steadiness, and Compliance. Take, for
example, Moses, who exhibited high Compliance in his
adherence to divine law and guidance, and David, whose
Dominant traits were deftly revealed in his assertive actions
against Goliath.

These figures were not merely products of their time but
embodiments of enduring human archetypes. Their lives offer a
canvas upon which today's personality theories, like the DISC
model, are superimposed, allowing for a convergence of time-
tested wisdom with current psychological practice
(Cunningham, 1992).

The tenets of wisdom found in the Bible can be seen as a precursor to the principles we use today to interpret human behavior. Just as Solomon's Influence shines in his diplomatic endeavors, modern leaders may express similar traits to navigate the complexities of governance and human relations (Popp et al., 2002).

Furthermore, the Steadiness of Joseph, exemplified through his service to Egypt despite tumultuous personal circumstances, speaks to the resilience and dependability taught in contemporary leadership practices.

Jesus Himself displayed all facets of the DISC profile: His Dominance in the temple with the money-changers, His Influence when feeding the multitudes and in His parables, His Steadiness in friendships, and His Compliance in fulfilling the prophecies and God's will. In this, one may find the perfect amalgamation of traits idealized in secular and sacred leadership.

Research in psychology has begun to affirm what ancient scripture has always suggested - that an individual's character is multifaceted and can reveal layers of complexity akin to what we now recognize in personality assessments (Glas, 1961).

Current disciples in both the ecclesial and psychological arenas must respect that the ancient texts hold insights into the wellsprings of human behavior. In the understanding of the self, one cannot overlook the possibility that scriptural figures were the early exemplars of traits we quantify today with instruments like the DISC assessment.

In this sense, the use of the DISC tool is not merely a modern imposition but, on the contrary, a continuation of an ancient intuitive understanding. Modern practice is not replacing ancient wisdom; rather, it is channeling it through new means, allowing us to glimpse the divine pattern imprinted upon humanity's heart.

When viewed through these lenses, biblical leadership styles are not at odds with contemporary notions of personality and temperament. Instead, they provide a foundation upon which modern methodologies can build - offering depth and context to discussions often confined to scientific domains.

The practical implications for those in ecclesiastic positions are expansive. Recognizing the continuity between ancient wisdom and modern practice means ensuring that the application of personality assessments such as DISC remains grounded in a perspective that honors the fullness of the human person as revealed through Christian anthropology (Matoon, 2020).

This can manifest in pastoral care, where understanding of DISC profiles can enhance the spiritual director's ability to guide others, speaking to their individual needs with a recognition of their intrinsic and God-given nature.

Moreover, embracing this continuity serves in the defense of a Christian understanding of the person against a tide of reductionist interpretations, asserting that the amalgamation of traits within an individual is reflective of divine complexity rather than mere psychological categorization.

In the end, the nuances of the DISC assessment, when placed alongside the tapestry of scripture, can act as a bridge between the ancient and the contemporary, granting insight into the enduring quest for self-understanding that is both a human desire and a God-given calling. It is a study of the soul that revels in truth, both contemporary and eternal.

The enduring utility of such wisdom cannot be overstated. For as the past informs the present, so too does the present shape the future. In bridging these worlds - the ancient and the modern - we forge a path illuminated by both the light of scientific inquiry and the glow of sacred revelation.

**Chapter 11: P-Types and Ancient Sinful Propensities**

In our progressive exploration into the vestibule of identity, "P-Types and Ancient Sinful Propensities" lays a cornerstone on which rests the parable of pathology observed through a prism of sanctity. Classical categorizations of personality often dance around the proclivity toward what ancient wisdom delineated as vice—yet these are not mere ethical aberrations, but rather signposts on the pilgrimage to virtue. By aligning the P-Types model within a Christian framework, we're reminded that each temperamental disposition, once baptized in grace, holds the potential to combat iniquity. Exegetes and neuropsychologists alike have illuminated the shadows cast by our fallen state, proposing that the cerebral architecture itself is inclined to sin's gravity (Fuller, 2022). Yet, amid this lacuna between fallible instinct and aspirational sanctity, the sacramental life emerges triumphant, as the embodiment of Christ's redemptive narrative in personal transformation (Nijoya, 1983). Thus, this chapter delves into the intersection of psychological predisposition and moral theology, offering a reconciliatory chorus of hope for those yearning to transcend the archetypal sins of our forebearers (Edinger, 1987).

**Personality and Pathology: A Biblical Interpretation**

The inquiry into the depths of human personality and its disorders must both capture the complexities inherent to our nature and be routed within a framework that echoes the divine order. As faith ventures beyond the seen towards the unseen, so must psychology stretch its understanding to the internal land that can't be traversed by mere empiricism. This begs us to contend with the conceptualizations of ancient sinful propensities, as personalities mirror the fractured aspects of our fallen nature.

The Biblical narrative provides a lens through which not only the traits of individuals but also the pathologies of the soul can be interpreted. The construct of P-Types in relation to ancient sinful propensities presents a nuanced methodology for understanding personality within the reverberating context of sin and redemption. Human pathologies are reminiscent of underlying sins, and therefore, the sacred text holds keys to the transformation from vice to virtue.

As we cross-examine personality disorders with scripture, it becomes apparent that these struggles aren't purely biological or environmental but are entangled with spiritual warfare (Ephesians 6:12). The persistent strain of pride within the human heart may manifest in the Narcissistic Personality

Disorder, unfurling as a flagrant disregard for others, and yet, one could find semblances of this pride within the Biblical narrative of the Tower of Babel, where human hubris sought to reach the heavens (Genesis 11:4).

Similarly, the pervasive sense of fear observed in those grappling with Anxiety Disorders can be seen as a lack of trust in divine providence, a theme poignantly illustrated through the incessant worry of Martha over the many tasks rather than choosing the good portion as Mary did (Luke 10:41-42). The Christian doctrine endorses casting all anxieties on a sovereign God, for He cares for His creation (1 Peter 5:7).

Depression, a common pathology in the present age, may be likened to the despondency of Elijah under the broom tree when he yearned for death (1 Kings 19:4). Yet, the story doesn't end in despair but in the gentle whisper of God guiding Elijah forward, emblematic of the restoration available through divine communion.

The impulsive and often detrimental decision-making in those with Borderline Personality Disorder resembles the impetuosity of Peter, whose emotional reactivity often precipitated regretful actions such as his emphatic denial of Christ (Matthew 26:74). Mercy, then, becomes a transformative agent that can heal impulsivity through steadfast love.

Whilst avoidance permeates the lives of those suffering from Avoidant Personality Disorder, the parable of the talents invokes the grave error in burying one's gifts out of fear (Matthew 25:25). Engagement, not retreat, is what the scripture advocates, as all are called to a life of fruitful stewardship.

The wrath that coloUrs the lives of those with Intermittent Explosive Disorder undeniably hearkens back to Cain's countenance falling before the slaying of Abel, a stark example of unchecked anger leading to demise (Genesis 4:5-8). A cautionary tale, it warns and instructs to master the sin that crouches at the door.

Historically, theologians have pondered how personality deformities reflect the brokenness of a world that groans for redemption (Romans 8:22). Disorders of the mind are then not exclusively cases for clinical intervention but also spiritual battlegrounds for grace-infused restoration.

The juxtaposition of these Biblical narratives against contemporary psychological pathologies underscores the inherent need for reconciliation with the Creator. Human pathology, when viewed through this paradigm, becomes a canvas displaying not only the scars of human fallibility but also the redemptive strokes of divine intervention.

The psychological community has produced significant insights into the nature of disorders afflicting the human psyche, insights which are neither to be dismissed nor undervalued. Yet, these must be held in tension with the ageless truths found in scripture. The Psalms especially speak to the innermost being, addressing sorrow, guilt, anger, and joy in ways that remain profoundly relevant to psychological discourse (Psalm 42:11).

Fundamentally, this scripturally informed interpretation of human pathology seeks to bridge the gap between the corporeal and the spiritual. It offers a perspective in which Christ's act of redemption is seen as the ultimate therapy – efficacious not only for the soul's salvation but also for the healing of the mind and emotions.

While the secular world may defer the origins of pathology to the natural realm, we must assert the spiritual dimension of these conditions. Redemption is an ongoing act which Christian doctrine proclaims reaches into all human experiences, including our mental and emotional struggles – not negating psychological science but beckoning it into the fuller light of truth.

It's in this pursuit that we find our convictions not only fortified but also our therapeutic approaches enriched. The Christian mental health professional esteems the dignity of the person fashioned by God while equally deploying scientific tools and insights in the alleviation of suffering.

This synthesis of sacred scripture and psychological science offers a framework by which we can understand and combat ancient sinful propensities within our personalities. It does so by acknowledging that while sin has frayed the fabric of human nature, grace possesses the power to reweave it into a tapestry that reflects the One who has made us in His image (Genesis 1:27).

**From Vice to Virtitude: Personal Growth in Christ**

In examining the transformation from vice to virtue, one must not overlook the profound interplay between personal constitution and divine grace. It's essential to consider the intrinsic human propensity towards certain transgressions, which have long been embedded within ancient doctrines and now resonate with contemporary psychological understanding. Within the Christian framework, this journey towards sanctification is navigated through the cultivation of virtues, as one endeavours to emulate the character of Christ.

Personal growth in Christ moves beyond mere self-improvement; it encapsulates a radical inner reformation that stems from the relationship with the divine. The Christian life is hence characterized by an ongoing process commonly referred to as theosis or divinization, whereby individuals become ever more Christ-like through cooperation with God's grace (Ware, 2003). This transformative process inevitably affects one's psychological and spiritual dimensions.

The underpinnings of vice can liken to flawed patterns in the tapestry of human personality. Sinful propensities may manifest as tangible personality tendencies, and their identification serves as the initial step towards rectification. The seven deadly sins - pride, greed, lust, envy, gluttony, wrath, and sloth - have a parallel in certain pathological personality types, which articulate a deeper spiritual malaise. However, within each vice lies the seed of a corresponding virtue - humility, generosity, chastity, kindness, temperance, patience, and diligence.

The church has long held that the cultivation of virtuous habits is the antidote to sinfulness (Aquinas, Summa Theologica). It's posited that these habits or virtues are to be fostered with intent and practice, as one might train the body or mind. For example, where pride seeks to elevate the self above others, humility grounds the soul in its true stature before God, acknowledging both its strengths and limitations.

Cognitive restructuring within a Christian context involves both recognition of sinful patterns and the deliberate alignment of thoughts with biblical truths. The psycho-spiritual techniques for developing virtues often lay in the practices of prayer, meditation, and scriptural reflection which rejuvenate the mind and reorient the heart towards God's will. These spiritual disciplines facilitate a realignment of personality quirks that once may have predisposed an individual towards vice, redirecting them towards virtuous living.

The narrative of personal growth is deeply entwined with community. Just as Christ modeled His life in fellowship with the disciples, believers are called to do life together (Hebrews

10:24-25). This shared journey provides mutual support and accountability, which significantly influences the maturation of character. The Apostle Paul's injunction to carry each other's burdens (Galatians 6:2) speaks not only to the act of assistance but also to the formative influence such communal life has on one's personality.

It is in the confession of sin and the experience of forgiveness that one discerns the tremendous impact of grace (Psalm 51). The acceptance of God's forgiveness is foundational to personal psychological healing and growth, as it dismantles the stronghold of guilt and shame that so often entrench individuals in self-destructive cycles (Walker, 2020).

The struggle against vice and the striving for virtue aren't meant to be attempts at moral perfectionism. Instead, they reflect an understanding of Christ's redemptive work which has already bridged the gap between flawed humanity and divine holiness. The Christian narrative accentuates that it is not through willpower alone that one undergoes this transformation but through the cooperative synergy between personal endeavor and divine assistance.

Empirical research within psychology suggests that personality traits are relatively stable, but evidence also points to the capacity for meaningful change, especially under significant life interventions such as religious conversion (Village & Francis, 2005). Personality, therefore, while having a baseline of stability, remains plastic to the formative touch of spiritual experiences and disciplines.

In the quest from vice to virtue, personal growth in Christ involves embracing one's identity as a new creation (2 Corinthians 5:17). The past proclivities towards sinful actions don't define the believer; rather, it is the newfound life in Christ that sets the trajectory for who they can become. This ontological shift undergirds the entire process of sanctification, rendering it not a self-imposed mandate but a divine covenant promise.

Forgiveness must be noted as a critical virtue in this transformative journey. It is both received from God and extended to others, which facilitates healing and reconciliation. The facet of forgiving as a psychological construct aligns closely with Christian teaching and has been shown to have significant mental health benefits (Worthington & Wade, 1999).

The role of the Holy Spirit cannot be overstated in this process of transformation from vice to virtue. As the Comforter and Guide, the Spirit convicts, counsels, and empowers individuals for righteous living, actualizing the inner renewal promised in scripture (Titus 3:5).

In summation, the transition from vice to virtue as posited in the Christian narrative is a complex interplay of personal effort and divine grace. It's a journey from the innate, sinful propensities of the human heart to a renewed, virtuous life modeled after Christ. The personal growth that ensues is marked by a deeper understanding of one's self in light of God's truth and a commitment to living out the virtues that reflect the divine nature.

**Chapter 12: Animal Symbols and Biblical Teaching (Smalley/Trent)**

Within the context of Christian anthropology, the vivid imagery of animal symbols provides a nuanced lens through which we might appreciate the intricacies of human personality. Smalley and Trent have captivated audiences by aligning certain animals—the Lion, Otter, Golden Retriever, and Beaver—with distinct personality traits. This symbolic association underpins much of Scriptural teaching, where animals are often employed metaphorically to impart spiritual insights.

The Biblical narrative is replete with creatures that encapsulate human characteristics. The lion, for example, symbolizes strength and leadership (Proverbs 28:1), traits that mirror a dominant personality within the Smalley and Trent typology. Yet, this archetype is not merely a secular understanding but rather finds its moorings in the Providence of the Creator, who endows individuals with such qualities for the edification of the body of faith.

Similarly, the otter, with its playful and sociable demeanor, subscribes to the communal aspect of Biblical teaching, harkening back to the Apostles' fellowship (Acts 2:42). Charm and buoyancy of spirits are reflections of a divine joy that all believers are called to embody.

Furthermore, the comparison to the Golden Retriever brings forth notions of loyalty and service, a direct parallel to the servanthood Christ exhibited and extolled (Mark 10:45). The steadfast nature of these individuals, much like the faithful animal, provides a living example of the steadfast love of the Lord (Lamentations 3:22).

Lastly, the Beaver, characterized by meticulousness and industriousness, mirrors the scriptural commendation to work heartily, as for the Lord (Colossians 3:23). It's in these methodical and diligent personalities that one can observe the confluence of divine ordination and human endeavor.

These animal metaphors serve as a guide, a blueprint of sorts, to acknowledge and cultivate the diverse gifts bestowed upon humanity. Just as Paul elucidates the diversity of gifts in 1 Corinthians 12, Smalley and Trent's animal symbolism illustrates practical expressions of these gifts, aiding individuals in understanding their unique calling within the shared mission of the Church.

In this vein, Scripture does more than inform; it transforms. The animal symbols and the personalities they represent are not static figures but dynamic agents for teaching and edification. By understanding the nature of these symbols within the Biblical context, one deepens not only self-awareness but also the capacity to partake in the narrative of salvation history.

This dual lens of looking at both the personality typology and its scriptural foundation allows for a holistic approach to character development. In the light of Revealed Truth, one sees not merely a behavioral pattern to be observed but a vocational call to be answered.

The practical implications of these symbolic associations extend beyond personal growth; they foster communal harmony. Recognizing the lion in leadership, the otter in fellowship, the Golden Retriever in pastoral care, and the Beaver in church administration or craftsmanship enriches the tapestry of church life, weaving together varying strands of personality into a cohesive whole that glorifies the Creator.

This theological perspective does not neglect the scientific understanding of personality but rather respects and integrates it. The rigors of psychological research, when seen through the lens of faith, can unveil the fingerprints of the Divine on the human psyche, and in doing so, advance our understanding of human nature and personality in profound ways (McGrath, 2011).

In conclusion, the intersection of animal symbolism and Biblical teaching provided by Smalley and Trent is not mere allegory or typological exercise; it is an invitation to embrace the fullness of one's God-given identity. Through this complementary approach, the faithful can explore the depths of psychology while remaining anchored in the immutable truth of Scripture. By doing so, they journey toward wholeness, sanctity, and the ultimate realization of their role in the divine plan.

**The Lion, Otter, Golden Retriever, and Beaver**

Within the realm of Christian anthropology, where the complexity of the human soul intertwines with the divine mystery, there emerges an intriguing parallel between animal symbols and human personality. Smalley and Trent's contribution to this conversation acts as an illuminating beacon that sheds light on individual temperaments through the lens of animal behaviors. It's here that the lion, otter, golden retriever, and beaver become more than mere fauna populating stories of the world; they become archetypes that reflect our intricately woven personalities.

The Lion, with its regal presence, symbolizes the natural leaders among us. Those who exhibit the qualities of a lion are often decisive, and commanding, showcasing a courage that energizes and mobilizes their surroundings (Smalley & Trent, 1989). In the scripture, we encounter lions in the context of strength and authority, resonating with those created in the image of an omnipotent God (Proverbs 30:30). It is this undeniable force of character that speaks to a certain segment of the faithful who find themselves drawn to leadership within the fold.

On the flip side of the symbolic spectrum lies the Otter, representative of the spontaneous and vivacious. Those akin to the otter embody exuberance and a joyous embrace of life's undulating tides (Smalley & Trent, 1989). In the Beatitudes, we find blessings for those who express a heartfelt zeal for existence, a pure reflection of the Creator's joy (Matthew 5:3-12). The Otter's spirit reflects a certain divine frolic, an invitation to participate in the playful dance of creation.

Contrastingly, the Golden Retriever represents loyalty and steadfastness – traits that are unwaveringly admirable. Those who share traits with this gentle dog are empathetic, patient, and deeply committed to the welfare of others (Smalley & Trent, 1989). Scripture frequently reminds us of the virtue of steadfast love, a cornerstone of our faith (1 Corinthians 13:7). The Golden Retriever personality reminds us of the call to embody unconditional love and support, mirroring the steadfastness of the Lord.

The Beaver, emblematic of the meticulous and orderly, shows us the value of structure and precision (Smalley & Trent, 1989). These individuals are typically methodical in their approach to life and work, exemplifying the Scriptural exhortations to use wisdom and prudence (Proverbs 14:8). Just as Solomon in all his wisdom constructed the Temple with great attention to detail, so does the Beaver personality teach us the significance of careful planning and execution in our earthly undertakings.

In analyzing these four distinct personalities through a biblical framework, it's imperative to acknowledge that each type holds both strengths and weaknesses – echoes of our post-Edenic nature, where virtues are often paired with inherent sinfulness. Yet, through the redeeming work of Christ, there is a purpose and place for each temperament within His divine plan (Romans 8:28).

The Lion's assertiveness, while noble, can sometimes verge on domineering, causing them to stray toward pride (Smalley & Trent, 1989). The scripture warns of the downfalls of pride and mandates humility (Proverbs 16:18). It's thus crucial for the Lion-like to constantly seek the guiding hand of the Divine, ensuring their strength is harnessed for righteous leadership.

Similarly, the Otter's vivacity can border on frivolity, leading them away from the weightier matters of faith and responsibility (Smalley & Trent, 1989). Here, scripture provides a counterbalance, urging joy to be paired with discernment and commitment to one's duties (Ecclesiastes 3:1-4).

The Golden Retriever's empathy could manifest in a reluctance to confront or an aversion to necessary change, potentially fostering a passive approach where action is required (Smalley & Trent, 1989). Scriptural wisdom teaches us to be "as shrewd

as snakes and as innocent as doves" (Matthew 10:16) —
balanced in our gentleness with a keenness to stand for truth.

The Beaver's orderliness, while commendable, can spiral into
rigidity, obscuring the gracious flexibility often required in
human relations (Smalley & Trent, 1989). The teachings of
Christ encourage us to embrace a new wineskin for new wine
(Mark 2:22), to be adaptable while maintaining a commitment
to excellence.

Through the understanding of these personality templates and
their alignment with scriptural truths, one can apprehend a
model for Christian growth. It is a journey towards
sanctification wherein one's innate temperament is refined and
aligned with the will of God. This transformative process does
not extinguish personality; rather, it elevates it to participate
more fully in the divine narrative.

Psychiatry may describe the psychological underpinnings of
these personality types, yet through the biblical lens, we find a
deeper ontology. The Lion, Otter, Golden Retriever, and Beaver
don't merely symbolize different modes of human behavior but
signify distinct paths through which the Imago Dei is expressed
and actualized in the world.

Such a theologically informed understanding of personality
evokes the recognition that these archetypes, though distinct,

are ultimately united in their source and aim. Just as the body of Christ is composed of varied members with different functions (1 Corinthians 12:12-27), so are the diverse temperaments meant to harmonize within the context of community and the greater good.

As we delve further into understanding the implications of these personality types, we are reminded that no one type is superior to another. Indeed, each finds its significance and redemption in the grand tapestry woven by the Creator Himself. To comprehend this is to see oneself as part of a divine mosaic, individuated yet part of a collective whole, unique yet undivided from the body of believers.

Ultimately, the Lion must learn the humility of servanthood, the Otter the substance of joy with purpose, the Golden Retriever the balance of love with truth, and the Beaver the harmony of order with grace. In doing so, we mirror the fullness of Christ – who embodies every virtue perfectly – and strive towards a personality that is not only psychologically sound but sanctified and glorifying to God.

Therefore, in embracing the metaphor of the Lion, Otter, Golden Retriever, and Beaver, the believer embarks on a path of contemplative reflection and active sanctification, discerning the ways one's God-given temperament can be a vessel for His work on Earth. In this sanctifying journey, personality and spirituality converge, bringing forth a discipleship that is as rich and varied as the animal kingdom itself, yet rooted in the singular love of our Creator.

## Animal Symbolism in Scripture and Personality Insights

In the intricate tapestry of biblical symbolism, animals hold a distinctive place, serving as metaphorical elucidations of human character traits and divine principles. The serpent in the Garden of Eden embodies deception while, in contrast, the lamb represents innocence and sacrifice (Ryken et al., 1998). So too do Smalley and Trent's analogies of the Lion, Otter, Golden Retriever, and Beaver offer profound lessons on our disposition and inclinations.

The Lion, often in scripture, signifies strength and authority. An individual likened to a Lion may display leadership and decisiveness, echoing the dominance of Judah from which the Messiah is prophesied to emerge (Genesis 49:9-10). It is a teaching of character one can't overlook, reflective not solely of brute force, but that of righteous governance, calling forth the Judaeo-Christian ethic of moral leadership.

Within the gaiety of the Otter, one finds parallels in the joys of the Psalms and the celebratory spirit present throughout Scriptural narratives. As the Otter is characterized by its playfulness and sociability, it's reminiscent of King David dancing before the Ark of the Covenant (2 Samuel 6:14). Here is a personality infused with a zest for life, evocative of the biblical injunction to "rejoice always" (1 Thessalonians 5:16).

The Golden Retriever, with its loyal and patient nature, represents the steadfast love and faithfulness so often praised in the Bible. The fidelity of Ruth or the patient endurance of Job typify these traits, as they are affirmed by one's companionship and resilience through adversity (Ruth 1:16; Job 1:21). These characters exemplify an innate drive for relational warmth and dedication.

Lastly, the industrious Beaver is captured in parables that commend diligence and wisdom, such as in the wise builder who constructs his house upon the rock (Matthew 7:24-27). Through the Beaver's meticulous nature, we witness a living metaphor for scriptural exhortations to thoughtful planning and unwavering effort.

Therein aligns our appreciation of personality with divine insight; each animal provides a mirror to our own soul and a window to understand others. In the ultimate wisdom of God's creation, including the minutiae of animal life, lies a reflection of our strengths, weaknesses, and the diverse ways we can serve the greater community.

This symbolism isn't simply archaic imagery but resonates deeply with the pervasive human quest for understanding the self. Psychologists have long recognized the correlation between personality types and behavioral patterns, which biblical personifications corroborate elegantly.

Such scriptural animal associations not only enrich our comprehension of sacred texts but also reinforce the ancient belief that all of creation is a lesson book teaching us about the Creator. They beckon us to a higher standard of self-awareness in our spiritual journey, just as the early Church fathers introspected to align their lives with the virtue and wisdom of Christ.

As we discern our own personalities through these animal symbols, we're invited to reflect on how these characteristics might manifest within our walk of faith. The lion-hearted may be called to leadership in church or society, whereas the otter-like joyfulness can serve to uplift the community in moments of sorrowful trials.

The Golden Retriever's emblematic loyalty prompts us to enduring commitment to faith and fellowship, serving as a cornerstone in both family and ecclesiastical contexts. In contrast, the Beaver's diligence equips us for disciplined study and fervent application of God's Word.

In our pursuit of self-awareness, it is crucial to remain humble and adaptable. The Bible cautions us against the sin of pride (Proverbs 16:18) and the erroneous belief in the incorruptibility of our judgment. The four animal symbols remind us of the plurality of gifts and the potential pitfalls of one-sided development.

Our analysis here is not to ascribe fixed destinies to individual temperaments but rather to discern the fluidity of God's grace in perfecting each unique disposition. Each biblical animal symbol serves as a lens through which we might see our personal transformation under God's sovereignty and mercy.

This awareness then, isn't for the glorification of the self, but for the edification of one's character and the Christian community. Understanding oneself becomes a path to greater empathy and service, in line with Christ's commandment to love one another (John 13:34-35).

The interaction between these personalities within the body of Christ represents the foundational narrative of scripture – unity in diversity. The mosaic of individualities within the church brings to fruition the Pauline vision of a body composed of many parts, each with its function and importance (1 Corinthians 12:12-27).

Embracing our personality, as mirrored by animal symbolism in Scripture, is to accept our role in the divine narrative. Each trait, each peculiarity, contributes to the grander scheme of God's salvific plan, as believers are refined like silver and tested like gold (Zechariah 13:9).

In summary, the study of animal symbolism within scripture offers profound insights into personality and human behavior. At the heart of this exploration lies an invitation to greater self-understanding, a call to service, and an affirmation of the divine image within each soul. Our personalities, in their multifaceted dimensions, are indeed instruments tuned by the Creator, meant to play harmoniously in the symphony of salvation history.

## Chapter 13: Four Species of Judaism and Christian Character

As we delve into this chapter, the goal remains steadfast: to illuminate the Christian character through the rich tapestry of Judaism, with a particular focus on the Four Species observed during the Feast of Tabernacles. These species—lulav (palm branch), etrog (citron), hadas (myrtle), and aravah (willow)—are not merely botanical elements; they possess deeply embedded psychological and spiritual connotations that resonate within the intricate fabric of personality (Neusner, 1995).

It is no coincidence that these species were chosen. Each carries a unique texture and scent, and when brought together, they symbolize the diverse attributes of personalities within the community of Israel and, by extension, the entire body of Christ. Let us consider the palpable nature of these species as it parallels the human constitution in dispositions, attitudes, and propensities of the soul.

The lulav, with its robust spine and vibrant fronds, stands as a metaphor for righteousness and internal fortitude. Like the spined palm, individuals who demonstrate strong character show forthrightness and an unwavering commitment to moral principles. They are piloted by an internal compass that points true north, despite the swirling winds of societal change and moral ambiguity. It is in the heart of such individuals that conviction and character find haven, much as the spine supports the palm (Goldstein & Goldstein, 1993).

In stark contrast, consider the etrog—a fruit of both fragrance and taste. It exemplifies those who possess not only the knowledge of God but also the fervor to affect their surroundings with the sweetness of good deeds. They approximate the words of the Apostle Paul, who implored believers to be the fragrance of Christ to God among those who are being saved and among those who are perishing (2 Corinthians 2:15). The etrog praises those who are wholesome in action and in piety (Goodman, 2004).

Moreover, the myrtle's small leaves, emitting perfume when crushed, evoke the character of resilience under pressure. For many believers, trials and tribulations serve not to diminish but to enhance their virtue, releasing the perfume of patience, long-suffering, and joy. This perseverance is not borne out of stoicism but from a vivacious faith in divine providence and the redemptive narrative espoused throughout Scripture. In their suffering, they do not become less, but more—like Christ in His passion.

The willow, distinguished by its simple, odorless leaves, symbolizes individuals who may lack the flamboyance of stronger personalities but contribute to the community through quiet, unwavering service. Their presence speaks to a character formed not in the spotlight, but in the shadows—faithful, dependable, seeking no acclaim but only to fulfill their role within God's economy.

Unity and diversity, then, are not merely encouraged but celebrated within the Christian character, embellished by the symbology of the Four Species. Each believer brings their distinctiveness to the common table, contributing to the sacred tapestry woven by the divine hand. It is in this rich diversity that the image of God shines forth, refracted through the prism of human personality into a multitude of colors and shades (Goldstein & Goldstein, 1993).

The Feast of Tabernacles itself is a time of joyous celebration of these differences, for in the coming together of the Four Species, the ritual invites reflection on the individual and collective journey towards holiness. The celebration is not merely a retrospective but a sanctified preparation, a calling to embody the future kingdom where divergent personalities converge into one harmonious doxology.

But the examination of these species in the light of Christian character reveals not just diversity but also a profound unity. As the species are bound together in the ritual, so too are individual characters bound in the unity of the Spirit. This unmistakable unity encompasses our varied psychological propensities, our distinct dispositions, aligning them with the ultimate will of the Creator (Neusner, 1995).

To overlook the significance of the Four Species within our reflection on Christian character is to neglect the rich Jewish heritage from which Christianity has sprung forth. By honoring and exploring this heritage, we gain deeper insights into the composition of our own faith and the diverse characters that populate our congregations.

Finally, the ritualistic binding of the Four Species encapsulates the call for believers to bind their own lives with that of Christ's, integrating their personality with His divine virtues. It is within this act of uniting that true Christian character is formed, shaped, and matured—an aspiration not just of the individual but of the collective unity of the Church.

Through this convergence of the Four Species and Christian character, this study invites contemplation upon the manner in which personality and faith interact, interfuse, and ultimately reveal a profound truth: that diversity creates not dissonance but harmony, and individual character traits, guided by divine revelation, manifest the very essence of the Kingdom of God. In doing so, we bear witness to a character that transcends the constraints of the mortal shell, reaching toward an eternal archetype that was, is, and ever shall be.

As we move forward in this discourse, let us retain the images of the Lulav, Etrog, Myrtle, and Willow, not just as botanical exemplars but as emblems of our spiritual and psychological ethos. In embracing these, we affirm our commitment to understanding the psychology of faith not as a nebulous concept, but as a lived reality, sanctified by tradition, scripture, and the indelible wisdom of the Creator (Goodman, 2004).

**Lulav, Etrog, Myrtle, and Willow: A Harvest of Personalities**

In the celebration of the Feast of Tabernacles, the Jewish tradition presents an elegant quartet of flora: the Lulav, Etrog, Myrtle, and Willow. Each of these species not only represents elements of the harvest but also, upon closer contemplation, mirrors a diversity of human personalities nested within the context of faith. It is through this contemplation that a discourse emerges, intertwining Biblical symbolism and the character of Christianity.

The Lulav, a palm branch standing erect, exudes an aura of righteousness and integrity. In the Christian ethos, such a personality aligns with an unswerving spirit - firm in convictions and soaring in aspirations. The Lulav reminds us of the steadfast who walk the path of truth, despite the desert winds of tribulation and temptation (Levitt, 2009).

The Etrog, citrus fruit, delicate with a beguiling scent, symbolizes those among us bearing the fruit of the Holy Spirit. It can't be overlooked how this echoes the call to be "fragrant offerings" (Ephesians 5:2), to live so as to spread the sweetness of virtue and the Gospel's refreshing zest.

In comparison, the Myrtle represents modesty with its petite, star-shaped leaves. Gazing upon it, one might contemplate the beatitudes, each leaf a gentle but insistent invitation to humility and peace-making -the quiet servants in the Kingdom whose gentle whispers echo through eternity (Matthew 5:3-12).

The Willow, with its leaves cascading toward the earth, mirrors the tears of the repentant and the empathetic cries of those who mourn. This personality type, within the Christian paradigm, highlights the irenic and compassionate individuals who grieve over sin and suffering, embodying the Savior's heart (Matthew 5:4).

These fractional insights into personality types find further resonance when coupled with an understanding of brain organization. Modern neuroscience posits that neuroplasticity reflects an interplay and potential adaptation of character traits (Begley, 2007). The brain, hence, like these four species, is pliable and capable of reflecting a spectrum of divine attributes.

Substantively, any exploration into character must remain lashed to the mast of Christian anthropology. Mankind, created imago Dei, is endowed with attributes reflective of the Divine but marred by the fall (Genesis 1:27, Romans 5:12). Thus personalities, like the Four Species, are at once potential instruments of virtue and vehicles for vice, each requiring cultivation and nurturing through grace and truth.

In assessment, the Four Species render a rich typology for meditation. Just as personality inventories attempt to codify human behaviors and inclinations, these species encapsulate the broad strokes of what could be deemed virtuous character traits, providing fodder for deep spiritual reflection within the Christian narrative.

Furthermore, this quartet transcends individualism, gesturing towards a greater unity. Each species, though distinct, is incomplete without the others. Similarly, St. Paul teaches that individual strengths contribute to the welfare of the Body of Christ (1 Corinthians 12:12-27), affirming the essential interconnectedness of our personal narratives.

While ancient, the Four Species maintain a pertinent vitality in encouraging a robust examination of what it means to flourish as humans and Christians. It is a synchrony that invites the faithful to bear fruit, to sway in the winds of the Spirit, to serve humbly, and to bend in compassionate sorrow and empathy.

Thus, this section's examination elicits contemplation into how these living symbols can harvest a character transformation. One doesn't only observe the Lulav, Etrog, Myrtle, and Willow but can deeply imbibe their existential and moral significance, guiding one's pathway to wholeness.

Complexities undeniably persist in correlating the biopsychological and spiritual dimensions. Yet, this marriage of thought enriches the endeavor of understanding and sanctifying the self in a world that increasingly marginalizes biblical anthropology. The Four Species, a verdant paradigm, direct contemplation towards an integral human identity, suffused with both diversity and unity.

In conclusion, this harvest of personalities becomes an apt metaphor for pastoral application. Clergy and counselors alike can draw from this paradigm, aiding individuals to appreciate their own and others' diverse contributions within the Christian community and the broader tapestry of human experience (Smith, 2011).

What lies at the heart of this discourse is a portrayal of the Christian life as both a solitary journey and a communal pilgrimage - a tapestry of personalities bound by common threads of faith, esperance, and caritas.

**Feast of Tabernacles: Celebrating Unity and Diversity**

In the Jewish tradition, the Feast of Tabernacles, also known as Sukkot, stands as a vibrant commemoration of unity amid diversity, a testament to both provision and protection experienced by the Israelites during their sojourn in the wilderness. Analogous to this eclectic celebration, the gathering 'Four Species' in Judaism metaphorically embodies the multiplicity and symbiosis within the Christian character.

The Four Species – lulav, etrog, myrtle, and willow – represent varied facets of nature. Each possesses its unique qualities yet combined, they signify the necessary integration of diverse spiritual attributes to achieve a harmonious and faithful life (Maimonides, 1180). This tenet can be transposed into the complexities of Christian anthropology, which postulates that the confluence of diverse traits forms a coherent identity in Christ.

The lulav, a palm branch, stands tall and straight, suggestive of the righteous who are upright in their convictions. It is emblematic of individuals who lead with strength and conviction, akin to the leadership typologies described in the DISC assessment. Its solidity and upward reach imply an unswerving connection to truth and a striving for divine standards.

In contrast, the etrog or citron, with its fragrant aroma and succulent taste, symbolizes those permeated with both learning and good deeds. Just as the etrog adds flavor, so can the intellectual and spiritual pursuits season the character, enriching it with depth and complexity. Psychologically, this parallels the cognitive functions detailed within the MBTI framework, where intuition and thinking fuse to foster a profound understanding of oneself and the cosmos.

The myrtle, with its sweet-smelling leaves, represents those who may lack scholarly learning but compensate richly in good deeds. Reflecting the FIRO-B emphasis on affection and inclusion, the myrtle resonates with the narrative of interconnectedness and altruistic service foregrounded in biblical relationships.

Suggestive of humility, the willow, with neither taste nor smell, exemplifies the unpretentious spirit, those content to operate without acclaim, much like the Golden Retriever personality in Smalley and Trent's animal symbolism typology. Often overlooked, it is this attribute which can steady and bind communities together.

In the Christian context, bringing these species together during the festival mirrors the apostle Paul's assertion that the church manifests as one body with many parts, each fulfilling a unique function (1 Corinthians 12:12-27). The cohesion of these varied elements translates to an ensemble of Christian characters that shape the multifaceted Christian community.

This amalgam of traits is not merely serendipitous; it reflects an orchestrated design, as the myriad of psychological assessments, from the Four Humors to the Enneagram, attests. Each system provides a scaffold for understanding the spectrum of human behaviors that map onto the diverse yet unitary body of Christ.

Tabernacles also heralds the eschatological hope, reminiscent of the harvest season. Every personality, as part of the collective harvest, contributes to the Kingdom's flourishing, anticipating the final ingathering where diversity is not merely tolerated but celebrated within unity (Zechariah 14:16).

Engaging with these typologies in light of the Feast of Tabernacles impels us to ponder the application of varied gifts in vocational discernment and ministry. Leveraging such diversity, individuals can function within the community authentically and synergistically, advocating a Christian anthropology that is not singular but plural, not monochrome but polychromatic.

Moreover, just as Sukkot involves dwelling in temporary shelters to remember Israel's dependency on God, Christians are reminded that their temporal personalities are mere vessels for eternal purposes. Each trait, each proclivity, and each temperament serves as a means to higher virtues and spiritual growth.

Yet, in this plurality, the potential for dissonance looms. The diversity that strengthens can also stratify. Hence, the alignment of the psychological paradigm with the biblical worldview necessitates an overarching governance of love and grace. In this governance, discordant characteristics harmonize, contributing to the sanctification of the individual and the community as a whole.

Psychiatry, while charting the pathologies of the mind, intersects with theology in the Feast of Tabernacles through a shared acknowledgment of the multifarious human condition, one that requires an integrative approach encompassing both spirit and psyche.

As we celebrate both unity and diversity, we recognize that the church does not call for uniformity. Instead, it nurtures a varied congregation where the convergence of the four species presents a vibrant tableau of what it means to be wholly human, wholly Christian, and wholly one in the body of Christ.

Thus, the Feast of Tabernacles stands as an enriching metaphor within this discourse, proposing a view of the human composition as beautifully complex, interdependent, and above all, reflective of divine creativity and intent.

**Chapter 14: The Gingerbread Cookie and the Hexaco Personality Model**

As we venture deeper into analyzing personality through both scientific models and biblical truth, we encounter the Hexaco Personality Inventory—a modern attempt to describe human dispositions. Those familiar with the model's dimensions—Honesty-Humility, Emotionality, Extraversion, Agreeableness, Conscientiousness, and Openness to Experience—might wonder how these categories resonate with the divinely inspired text of Scripture (Ashton & Lee, 2007).

The parallels begin with the Humility-Honesty trait, which recalls the Sermon on the Mount, where the humble and the pure in heart are blessed (Matthew 5:3-12). This trait encapsulates a disposition towards fairness, sincerity, and modesty—a reflection of the Christ-like character. Indeed, humility is not merely a virtue but a fundamental orientation of the soul towards God, and honest dealings are emblematic of the heart transformed by grace.

Emotionality in the Hexaco model brings to mind the psalmist's deep well of feelings and affective expressions towards God. By acknowledging our 'fearfully and wonderfully made' emotions (Psalm 139:14), we affirm that emotional depth is not antithetical to the biblical worldview but rather integral to the relational fabric with the Divine and the community of believers.

Extraversion, with its characteristic energy and social engagement, parallels the call of the apostles to be a light unto the world (Matthew 5:14). Such outward-looking zest does not eclipse the interior life; instead, it is its natural expression, as extolled in the varied ways members of the early Church engaged with one another (Acts 2:42-47).

Agreeableness, as described in scientific parlance, echoes the apostolic exhortations to live in harmony with one another, showing empathy and understanding (Romans 12:16). It underscores the biblical admonition to 'bear one another's burdens' (Galatians 6:2) and to embody the love that 'is patient and kind' (1 Corinthians 13:4).

Conscientiousness, with its emphasis on diligence and reliability, aligns with the wisdom writer's celebration of a disciplined life (Proverbs 12:24). It is also resonant with the parables of Jesus, which often hold the faithful and wise servant as exemplary (Matthew 24:45-51).

Openness to Experience, while it may seem at odds with traditionalism, actually reflects the biblical narrative that periodically involves radical shifts in understanding God's will and purpose (Acts 10:9-16). Like Peter, openness allows us to perceive new truths and to appreciate the manifold beauty of God's creation, as well as diverse ways of perceiving His work.

Combined, these traits present a complex gingerbread cookie, sweetened by divine intention and spiced by human frailty. As is the case with baking, the right proportions matter. Too much of one spice can overwhelm the palate, metaphorically speaking, while too little may render the flavor bland and indiscernible.

The Hexaco model, in this light, serves as an empirical confirmation of the complex nature of humanity as described in Scripture. It provides a lexical framework to describe personality dimensions that are deeply anchored in the Judeo-Christian narrative (Ashton & Lee, 2007).

Yet, the idea of personality is incomplete without addressing the aspect of sin, which has introduced a distortion, a crack in the immaculate design. Like a gingerbread cookie that's been chipped, our brokenness is apparent. Since the Fall, the traits intended for harmonious living have been bent towards self-serving ends, with pride often supplanting humility and deceit disguising as honesty.

Understanding personality through this model can lead one on a journey of self-awareness and growth. Recognizing one's weaknesses and proclivities towards sin does not confine or condemn; rather, it illuminates paths towards redemption and sanctification, paths that are laid out in Scripture and actualized through the power of the Holy Spirit.

The redemptive narrative is hence not only about escaping sin but about realigning these personality traits towards their original divine purpose. Honesty and humility are restored in repentance, emotionality in genuine worship, extraversion in service, agreeableness in community, conscientiousness in stewardship, and openness to God's ever-unfolding revelations.

In the ongoing culinary allegory, God can be seen as the master baker, one who does not discard the broken cookie but instead crafts a new creation. Each trait, each spice, is measured again, restored, and perfected through Christ, who redeems both the form and the substance of our humanity.

This inquiry into the Hexaco model within a Christian framework underlines the hope of the gospel—that through the acknowledgment and understanding of our fractured nature, we find the potential for divine restoration. As we shape our lives and personalities according to biblical truth, we move ever closer to realizing the 'imago Dei' inherent within us.

In summary, the Hexaco model, when viewed through the lens of Christian theology, provides a valuable vocabulary for discussing personality with both scientific and philosophical precision. It can bolster our comprehension of human nature

and facilitate our journey towards Christ-like transformation
(Ashton et al., 2007).

**Honesty-Humility, Emotionality, and others through
Biblical Examples**

In scrutinizing the Hexaco personality model within a biblical
framework, one becomes increasingly aware of the resonances
between this contemporary typology and the age-old wisdom
found in Scripture. The model's dimension of Honesty-Humility
is underscored by the prima facie simplicity yet underlying
complexity of figures such as Joseph of Arimathea, who, amid
societal pressures, courageously and humbly claimed the body
of Christ for burial (Mark 15:43-46). Joseph exemplifies the
unfeigned humility and honesty of heart that destines the soul to
be elevated to the heights of divine intimacy.

The inscription of Emotionality within the Hexaco paradigm
mirrors the passionate intensity of King David, a man whose
psalms are soaked with the timbre of raw human emotion.
David's experiences, conveyed in his poetic laments and
exultations, demonstrate the depth of feeling that is not an
aberration from divine likeness but a feature of the image
imprinted upon humanity by its Creator (Psalm 6:6-9).

Focusing on the dimension of eXtraversion, one can discern its
traits in the Apostle Peter. His impulsive disposition and
outspoken demeanor, although occasionally leading him astray,
were forged through the crucible of grace into the rock upon

which the Church was established (Matthew 16:18). Peter's transformation reveals how personality, directed by the divine hand, can be channeled into the service of a cause surpassing human ambition.

Agreeableness in Hexaco finds its reflection in the archetypal figure of Ruth, whose kindred loyalty and amiable nature illustrate how relational affinity and compassion align one with the will of God even through the most grief-stricken chapters of life (Ruth 1:16-17).

As for Conscientiousness, the biblical character of Daniel serves as an eminent exemplar. Amidst a den of corruption, Daniel's unwavering adherence to prudence, discipline, and ethical conviction showed forth in his resistance to defilement (Daniel 1:8), even when his steadfastness cast him into a literal den, from which his integrity was vindicated (Daniel 6:22).

In the arena of Openness to Experience, Solomon's earnest petition for divine wisdom and his subsequent rule, hallmarked by philosophical contemplation and an appreciation for the natural world, illustrate how openness acts as a conduit for the revelation of divine truths (1 Kings 4:29-34).

These archetypes, portrayed in flesh and blood within the tome of the Bible, are not mere allegories for virtuous conduct; they are testaments to the interplay between divine providence and human personality in the drama of salvation history. Each figure mentioned faced their own intrinsic inclinations, positively and negatively, and yet through divine grace, their personalities contributed to God's salvific plan.

Indeed, personality is not a static mold but a dynamic medley of traits that, in the confines of fallen nature, can succumb to vice or, in the light of grace, can ascend to virtue. Abraham's lie about the identity of his wife Sarah demonstrates how even those with a trajectory towards righteousness can falter when honesty is compromised (Genesis 12:11-13).

Conversely, the intense emotional spectrum can have destructive consequences, as evidenced by Saul's jealousy towards David, which led to oppressive behaviors (1 Samuel 18:8-9). Despite the potential for emotionality to engender empathy and connection, it can also gestate envy and malcontent, illustrating the necessity of temperance.

Extraversion, while often associated with leadership and discipleship, can also precipitate brashness, as seen when Peter denied Christ thrice (Luke 22:54-62). Though later restored, Peter's failure underscores the need for self-restraint and reflective prudence in the harnessing of one's outward energies.

Furthermore, the agreeable nature can be swayed into complacency, as Ananias and Sapphira tragically demonstrated through their deceit born out of an eagerness to please the community, which led to their downfall (Acts 5:1-11). Their demise serves as a stern caveat about the interplay of personality and moral choice.

Again, conscientiousness, devoid of flexibility, risks becoming obstinacy, as in the case of the Pharisees whose scrupulous adherence to tradition blinded them to the new covenant Christ was offering (Matthew 23:23-24).

Openness to new experiences, unmoored from truth, can lead to idolatry and moral confusion, as Solomon himself later displayed by allowing foreign influences to compromise his dedication to God (1 Kings 11:1-8).

In examining such characters and traits, we witness a duality within the human form: the capacity for transcendence and the propensity for degradation. Within this spectrum, the individual is called to navigate the interstices of virtue and vice, employing personality not as the determinant of destiny but rather as the instrument through which one might, with divine assistance, cultivate a soul reflecting the full radiance of creation's original intent.

Thus, the Hexaco model, when viewed through the scripture's multivalent lens, offers not only a psychological profile but also a road map for sanctification. The personality, as a unique amalgamation of divine image and earthly clay, bestows upon each person the task of coauthoring with the Creator the unfolding story of redemption.

**Humanity Baked in Sin and Redeemed for Goodness** The syllogism that integrates sin and redemption within the very fabric of humanity permits an examination not solely at a theological level but through the discerning lenses of psychology and anthropology. To chart this ontology, we begin with the inherent flaw that is original sin, an inextricable thread woven into humanity's very essence. At the same time, an antithetical but equally robust thread runs parallel—redemption and the propensity toward goodness, a narrative deeply embedded within the Christian doctrine.

The narrative of humanity's fall and subsequent redemption permeates Biblical tradition, reflecting a tapestry rich in hues of moral and psychological complexity. As humankind inherits the burden of sin, so too do they bear the potential for salvation, a concept inextricable from the Christian understanding of personhood. The binary between vice and virtue, as underscored by a biblical worldview, is not merely didactic; it lays the foundation upon which human morality is assessed and understood (Smith, 2019).

From this perspective, the concept of sin is not solely a marker of ethical failure but becomes a starting point for psychological exploration. Sinful behaviors, emotions, and tendencies are, in essence, deviations from the archetypal form of the Imago Dei in which humanity was created. This divergence from the original nature bestowed upon human beings serves as a testament to the flaw inherent in the human condition, one that necessitates divine intervention for its rectification (Jones, 2021).

Redemption, then, is conceptualized as the process of returning to one's original goodness, a reclamation of the divine spark within. It is within this framework that Christian anthropology contends with the duality of man: a creature marked by sin yet perpetually called to a higher standard of moral excellence. It is a dialectic that must be managed, rather than resolved, for it resides at the very heart of human existence (Martin et al., 2018).

The Hexaco personality model, with its emphasis on honesty-humility, emotionality, extroversion, agreeableness, conscientiousness, and openness to experience, creates a multifaceted framework through which one may discern elements of the Divine entwined with our fallen nature. The inclusion of the honesty-humility dimension introduces a moral and ethical component to personality assessment that dovetails neatly with the theological construct of original sin (Ashton & Lee, 2007).

Through the prism of Hexaco, we see how the interplay between our inherent flaws and the bestowed virtues represent the battleground of the human soul. Honesty and humility are qualities that align closely with the Christian virtue of humility, which opposes the pride that is often deemed the root of all sin. Emotionality can be seen akin to the passion of Christ, a reflection of both human frailty and divine empathy (Ashton & Lee, 2007).

The domain of extroversion within the Hexaco model encapsulates our need for communion, both with our fellow humans and with the divine. Christianity herself is a religion of relationship, eternally gesturing towards the other in quest of authentic connection. Agreeableness suggests a proclivity towards forgiveness, echoing Christ's call for mercy. Conscientiousness aligns with the tenacity required for a life lived in adherence to divine law, while openness to experience embraces the transformative journey of sanctification.

Sin presents itself as an aberration in these traits that can steer individuals from their divine path. The Christian narrative does not leave us stranded at the recognition of these aberrations but offers a pathway to realign through the sacraments, scriptural exhortations, and the active pursuit of virtue. Redemption—the fulcrum of the Christian message—is both the hope and the blueprint for restoring the architecture of the soul to its original design (Martin et al., 2018).

This constant flux between sin and redemption can be traced within our neurology and comportment. From the brain's neuroplasticity to the heart's inclinations, the potential for moral and psychological transformation is a testimony to the grace that saturates human existence. It underlines the belief that even the most sinful of characters retain the capacity for redemption, that no individual is beyond the reach of sanctification (Jones, 2021).

The implications of this dual nature extend to the practice of psychiatry and the broader context of mental health. While secular modalities may seek to remediate psychological dysfunction purely through empirical methods, a biblical approach takes into account the soul's plight, acknowledging the need for spiritual as well as psychological healing. This intercession posits that true wellness encompasses a redemptive trajectory that culminates in the restoration of one's relationship with God and their inherent goodness (Smith, 2019).

It becomes apparent, then, that humanity's struggle with sin is not simply a theological construct but a lived psychological reality. The enduring principles of Christian anthropology serve not only to illuminate the path of the fallen but also to provide the necessary means for their elevation. In essence, the quest for goodness within a fallen world is one that encompasses every dimension of the human experience, imploring an integrative approach toward holiness.

In conclusion, humanity, though 'baked in sin', is perpetually invited to partake in the redemptive love of the Creator. The Hexaco model lends itself as a tool for reflection, allowing one to explore the areas in which they may have diverged from the path of goodness and to devise strategies for realignment. Psychological models and typologies when interpreted through the prism of Christianity, don't merely categorize personalities but illuminate the road to salvation.

**Chapter 15: Enneagram: A Road to Spiritual Conversion**

As we tread the pathway of self-discovery and spiritual growth, the Enneagram serves as a map, illuminating the terrain of the human soul with profound precision. This ancient tool, when understood within the context of Christian anthropology, offers a dynamic framework for spiritual conversion, observing not merely the superficiality of behaviors but the undercurrents of motivation that give rise to actions.

Indeed, the Enneagram teaches us that there are nine primary personality types, and within these types, there exist a triad of instincts—self-preservation, social, and sexual (or one-to-one)—that influence our behavior (Riso & Hudson, 1999). These personality patterns can serve as both lenses through which we view the world and prisons that can bind us to sin, should we remain unaware and unchanged.

The spiritual journey through the lens of the Enneagram starts by identifying one's type, which reveals not only one's virtues but also one's vices. This self-awareness is paramount in Christian life, as it echoes the call to know oneself—'gnōthi seauton'—a principle which, while predating Christianity, was embraced by the Church Fathers as essential for spiritual growth (Palmer & Brown, 1997).

Each Enneagram type has a unique path to healing and wholeness, reflecting the diverse pathways of conversion depicted in Scripture. The fear-driven actions of a Type Six, for example, may find solace in the biblical admonition to trust in Divine Providence, while the pride of a Type Two could be humbled through Christ's example of servant leadership.

The role of confession and repentance is magnified when we view sin through the Enneagram's lens; each type's specific challenges become areas for targeted spiritual warfare and confession, rather than a generic and unfocused sense of guilt.

Moreover, the Enneagram illuminates the capital sins traditionally upheld by Christian teaching—pride, envy, wrath, sloth, greed, gluttony, and lust. Each type wrestles with a particular sin more acutely, providing a tailored strategy for spiritual combat to attain the opposing virtue (Naranjo, 1990).

Moving forward, one must heed the Enneagram's warning against using it as a tool for self-justification rather than transformation. Without a steadfast commitment to spiritual conversion, the Enneagram can easily become an excuse to wallow in one's failings, misdirecting us from the essence of the Gospel—the transformative power of Christ's love.

Engagement with the Enneagram also fosters compassion within the Christian community. As we learn to see the world through each other's eyes, we gain a deeper understanding of each member's unique struggles and gifts. This insight paves the way for more effective ministry as we cater to the distinct needs of each personality type in the Body of Christ.

Furthermore, the resurrection narrative provides the ultimate foundation for this transformative journey. As the Enneagram points out our false identities and sin patterns, the power of the Resurrection promises not just a reformation but a complete rebirth, projecting our true identity in Christ.

In the act of spiritual conversion, the Christian must move beyond mere intellectual assent to the teaching of the Enneagram. It requires an embracing of daily practices such as prayer, meditation, and community life, which are rooted in the context of a lived-out faith that transforms character and promotes sanctification.

We see, then, that the Enneagram is not only a psychological tool but a spiritual one, calling us to a higher plane of existence where our human potential is realized through the grace of God. It calls us to a journey that is not solitary but one that we undertake within the community of believers.

Let us conclude this chapter by affirming that our ultimate goal is not simply self-knowledge or self-improvement but the pursuit of holiness. Through the Enneagram, we walk the narrow road, where each type unveils a unique way of bearing the image of God, and each path converges at the foot of the Cross, where all are made new.

**Types and Triads: Finding Oneself in the Salvation Story**

The Enneagram, an ancient symbol with its roots entwined in mystical traditions, has been resurrected in contemporary times as a tool for self-understanding and spiritual growth. At its core, the Enneagram posits that there are nine distinct personality types, each with its own motivations, fears, and potentialities. In this context, it becomes a transformative mirror reflecting our deepest selves against the backdrop of the grand salvation narrative.

Each of the nine points of the Enneagram is associated with a particular type of person, distinguished by unique attributes and tendencies. As a triadic structure, it encompasses three groups of types that correspond to the centers of human intelligence: the instinctive, the feeling, and the thinking centers. This trifurcation is essential to discerning how individuals can navigate their paths and participate authentically in the Christian saga of redemption.

Crucially, the scriptural paradigm teaches that humanity is made in the divine image, yet marred by sin, and thus, each personality type also embodies a distinct pathway towards or away from virtues and vices (Riso & Hudson, 1999). It is within this framework that the Enneagram can serve as a beacon to guide individuals towards the virtues of faith, hope, and love, which stand as the bedrock of Christian living.

This typology is not static; it interacts dynamically with an individual's growth and progression on their spiritual journey. One's basic type persists, but the way it is expressed can change radically. Such fluidity reflects not only psychological development but also the profound impact of grace and conversion in a person's life.

The instinctual triad, encompassing Types One, Eight, and Nine, identifies those whose primary responses to life are grounded in the body; they may struggle with issues of anger and autonomy, but also have the potential for great courage and magnanimity. As one discovers their place within this triad, it beckons a reflection on Christ cleansing the temple (John 2:13-16), an act emblematic of righteous anger harnessed for holy purpose.

The heart or feeling triad, consisting of Types Two, Three, and Four, grapples with identity and the need for appreciation. These types are primed to cultivate empathy, altruism, and authenticity, as long as vanity and deceit do not overtake them. Consider Judas Iscariot, whose desire for recognition may have pushed him over the edge into betrayal (Matthew 26:14-16).

Those in the thinking triad, Types Five, Six, and Seven, are characterized by their search for security and truth. While their gifts include wisdom and foresight, they must be wary of succumbing to fear and acedia. The apostle Thomas, with his doubting yet analytical mind, provides a biblical figure with whom the thinking triad could identify and learn from (John 20:24-29).

Understanding the Enneagram's type structure is merely the beginning. One must also consider the wings and the lines of integration or disintegration which suggest pathways of stress and growth. Like Paul's transformation on the road to Damascus (Acts 9:1-19), a person can exhibit shifts towards less habitual behaviors when encountering God's grace or the stressors of life.

Moreover, the triadic arrangement posits that no one is purely one type, and the interconnectivity of types points towards the compassion and complexity imbued in the tapestry of human relationships. This echoes the Pauline epistles, wherein the apostle speaks of the body of Christ as a unity of different parts, each essential and interdependent (1 Corinthians 12:12-27).

In the spiritual pilgrimage, self-awareness is a key step towards redemption. The parable of the Prodigal Son (Luke 15:11-32) encapsulates this, showing a journey from self-indulgence to self-knowledge and a return to right relationship with the father. Similarly, the Enneagram aids in the discernment of one's sins and shortcomings, but more importantly, one's redemptive capacities as a child of God.

When guided by the insights of the Enneagram, one is not merely decoding a psychological framework but engaging with a spiritual tutor that enlightens the path towards divine resemblance. The types elucidate why we traverse different paths in our approach to God, yet those very paths can converge at the foot of the cross—a union in Christ's redemptive act.

It is in realizing and accepting the multifaceted structure of the human soul, as the Enneagram illustrates, that one can more deeply understand personal vocation and communal sanctification. The types serve as reminders that the call to holiness is universal, yet the response to that call is peculiar to each individual story embedded in Christ's salvific narrative.

Thus, as we explore Types and Triads through the Enneagram, as Romans so aptly teaches, we recognize that we are all "conformed to the image of His Son" (Romans 8:29). In this sacred journey, the Enneagram illuminates our unique footprint within the vast salvation story, urging us toward spiritual conversion—one that redeems our type-specific frailties into glorious reflections of the Creator's image.

Though the Enneagram is a tool originating from sources outside the directly revealed truth of Scripture, it can nevertheless be appropriated within a Christian framework. When employed wisely and discerningly, it is one of many instruments in the service of spiritual formation, a means to foster the personal and collective embodiment of Christ-like love (Riso & Hudson, 1999).

**Enneagram and the Call to Holiness in Christian Life**

In the journey toward spiritual maturity, the Enneagram serves as a profound tool for introspection and transformation within the Christian paradigm. When engaged with discernment, it becomes more than a mere map of personality; it evolves into a dynamic compass guiding the faithful towards the zenith of holiness. The quest for sanctity is intrinsic to the Christian vocation, and the Enneagram facilitates a piercing examination of conscience that is crucial to this pilgrimage (Merton, 1960).

The premise of the Enneagram intersects with the underlying Christian doctrine that human beings are inherently inclined towards sin, but are simultaneously offered the grace of redemption. This tool does not operate outside the penumbra of faith but illuminates the specifics of one's personal rendezvous with sin and grace. It underscores nine distinct paths of spiritual ascent and descent that correspond to fundamental dispositions and inclinations of the human heart (Rohr & Ebert, 2001).

The Enneagram's structure, encompassing nine personality types, mirrors the Christian notion that diversity is woven into the fabric of creation. Each type reflects a distinct aspect of God's image, highlighting that variety does not imply disunity but rather complements the collective journey to holiness. The diversification of pathways illuminated by the Enneagram recognizes the individual narrative within the grand story of salvation (Palmer, 1991).

To embark on this pilgrimage of sanctification with the guidance of the Enneagram, one must first dwell in authentic self-awareness. It is a tenet of Christian spirituality that true knowledge of self leads to deeper knowledge of God. In this light, the Enneagram offers a mirror to the soul, revealing both the virtues and the vices nestled within one's character. It calls attention to the particular fortresses within which pride hides and the unique expressions of the seven deadly sins in individual conduct.

However, Christian life is not merely about the recognition of sinfulness; it is predominantly about the embrace of divine mercy and grace. The Enneagram is not to be a prison of self-identification but rather a springboard for grace-filled transformation. Each type offers insights into the pathways by which the Holy Spirit may most effectively sanctify the individual soul. For example, where Type One individuals may find sanctification through embracing mercy over perfectionism, a Type Seven may journey toward holiness through temperance and gratitude (Zuercher, 1992).

The dimension of spiritual growth is emphasized when Enneagram insights are aligned with prayer, sacraments, and community life—foundational elements of Christian practice. Here, each Enneagram type discerns its unique fragilities and gifts in the context of a greater ecclesial body. The community becomes a rich tapestry of personal struggles and triumphs, collectively nurturing the embodiment of Christ's presence in the world (Plante, 2009).

The role of the spiritual director or confessor is pivotal in interpreting the revelations of the Enneagram within the bounds of Christian theology. Guided by ecclesiastical wisdom, the Enneagram becomes an invaluable confidant in the soul's confession. It is in confession that the stark illumination of one's flaws meets the inexhaustible mercy of God, and the Enneagram can serve to bring clarity and focus to this sacrament.

Moreover, the call to holiness in Christian life is intimately interwoven with the cultivation of virtues, and the Enneagram has a role to play here as well. Each type naturally gravitates toward certain virtues and struggles with their opposing vices. A nuanced understanding of these tendencies empowers individuals to pursue the virtues that align with their divine calling (Chestnut, 2013).

Christ's exhortation to the pursuit of perfection, as the Heavenly Father is perfect, gains newfound depth through the Enneagram's elucidation. Holiness does not entail a monochrome existence but blossoms fully in the variegated garden of human personalities. The Enneagram underscores that the journey to holiness is uniquely tailored to the spiritual topography of each soul.

As each type on the Enneagram possesses a shadow side — the underbelly of sin that can cause one to stray from God's law — there also lies the potential to illuminate Christlike virtues. For instance, where Type Three's may grapple with deceit and vanity, their sanctified calling urges them towards authenticity and altruism reflecting the servanthood of Christ.

In the realm of discipleship and Christian service, the Enneagram aids practitioners in understanding their natural inclinations towards certain ministries. Recognizing one's inherent gifts and the corresponding challenges paves the way for more effective and passionate service to God and one's neighbors, fulfilling the two greatest commandments Christ himself identified.

When applied with rigor and in alignment with Scripture, the Enneagram transcends its roots in ancient wisdom, becoming a beacon of introspection in the modern Christian life. It fosters a continuous conversion of heart — metanoia — which is at the heart of the Gospel message. The Enneagram thus propels believers not towards self-obsession but towards self-forgetfulness, in the pursuit of the One who calls each by name (Luke 19:9).

In conclusion, the Enneagram, within the context of Christian spirituality, acts as an incisive tool complementing the lifelong vocation to holiness. It provides a tailored diagnostic of the soul's maladies and prescribes a corresponding regimen for spiritual health that aligns with God's redemptive work within the tapestry of the Church. Fundamentally, it resonates with the scriptural admonition to assess and renew one's mind and heart, aligning with the ultimate purpose for which humanity was created — to abundantly reflect the glory of God (Ephesians 4:22-24).

## Conclusion

In the discourse of character and consciousness, science and scripture have not always journeyed hand in hand. This treatise has ventured to dispel the estrangement, decoding the tapestry of personality through the gestalt of biblical wisdom and psychological inquiry. The synthesis achieved here presents not merely an alignment but an intricate interrelation, whereby the study of typologies is vivified by theological insights, culminating in a holistic understanding of the human person.

The exploration of divergent personality frameworks has offered a panoramic view, and within this vista, revealed truth has not stood as a mere spectator. Rather, it has infused the typological analysis with profundity, guiding us toward a recognition of the Imago Dei embedded within our complex neurobiological and psychological make-up. An embrace of this composite vision amplifies our comprehension of self, others, and the sovereign narrative in which we partake.

Morality, a construct both scrutinized and celebrated, finds its surest footing when grounded in the rich soil of Christian anthropology. As we have navigated the contours of each personality typology, we have encountered the fact that virtue and vice are not arbitrary opposites but dynamic factors shaping our journey towards sanctification. Each idiosyncrasy, each temperamental nuance, can be channelled towards that process of becoming more fully human, more fully divine.

Furthermore, in cross-examining typologies with the biblical account of human nature, we unlock a more profound wisdom in our pursuit of psychological health. The various methodologies, from FIRO-B to the Enneagram, have revealed themselves as not merely diagnostic tools but as roadmaps for spiritual maturity. The narratives and parables of scripture breathe life into these frameworks, endowing them with purpose and direction.

Our investigation into Type A and Type B personalities elucidates the interplay between action and contemplation, mirrored in the lives of Martha and Mary, reminding us of the necessary balance critical to the Christian walk. Similarly, the investigation into the four humors speaks volumes to the diversification of gifts and the collective synergy within the body of Christ (Smith & Jones, 2021). The admonition is clear: the singular member cannot say to the body, "I need thee not," for in each persona lies an indispensable thread in the divine tapestry.

The Jungian archetypes, aligned with biblical figures, underscore the narrative that we are each part of a cosmic drama, our roles replete with both shadows and light. Understanding this duality soothes the soul's disquiet, steering us towards integration and authenticity. Likewise, the Myers-Briggs typology does not merely pigeonhole but propels individuals towards discernment of vocation, encouraging the cultivation of inclinations that harmonize with the Creator's intent.

In this journey, we have learned that personality is not a static marker but a dynamic interplay of tendencies that draws us towards deeper self-awareness and transformation. The DISC assessment, aligned with biblical leadership styles, urges a wise stewardship of our natural dispositions in service to the Gospel.

The conjunction of moral vices with the P-Types, or the correspondence of animal symbols with biblical teaching, accentuates the anthropological premise of sin and redemption woven within our very being. These models are not mere psychological curios but speak to the persistent human question of transformation from vice to virtue – the Pauline metamorphosis from old man to new creation (Smith et al., 2020).

The mirthful symmetry found in the Four Species of Judaism brings a celebratory lens to our character typologies, just as the Harvest feast harmonizes diverse elements into a unified whole. The Gingerbread Cookie model illustrates our quirks and complexities, illustrating a panorama of character traits redeemed and hewn into a portrait of sanctified humanity.

The Enneagram model has been proffered as a spiritual tool for self-examination and growth, patterning a course of conversion aligned with our fervent pursuit of holiness. These enneatypes, much like the beatitudes, counsel the soul in its ascent, molding the contours of character in consonance with divine grace.

In sum, our contemplation of personality through the prism of Scripture has not been an endeavor in reductionism. On the contrary, the religious dimension enhances our understanding of personality by providing a teleological perspective that grounds morality in the inherent and transcendent dignity of the human person (Jones, 2022). Each personality type, when viewed through the lens of faith, takes on an eternal dimension, pointing to our ultimate end: union with the divine.

Thus, we affirm that the nexus of psychology and theology offers a more enriched, nuanced understanding of the human person. Our excursions into typologies illumined by Scripture's lantern attest to an eternal truth: that every human heart is a palimpsest, bearing the image of the Creator and inscribed with the narrative of salvation. It is in recognizing and embracing this narrative that one may walk the path to wholeness and sanctity.

As we close the pages of this discourse, may we carry forward the conviction that psychology and Christian anthropology are not adversaries but allies in deciphering the enigma of human existence. As we continue to integrate revealed truth into our understanding of the psyche, we inch closer to the horizon where divine Wisdom kisses earthly knowledge, where the soul finds rest in the plenitude of truth.

**The Synthesis of Typology and Theology: A Holistic View**

In the consideration of typology and theology, an integrative approach is not only desirable but essential. This synthesis is the cornerstone of our concluding reflections, as it marries the inherent complexity of human personality with the profound depths of theological truth. To see man solely through the lens of typology without the illumination of sacred theology would be akin to studying the cosmos without the light of the stars.

The exploration of personality typologies across various psychological frameworks has opened a diverse spectrum of understanding, reflecting the dynamic nature of our created being. However, it is in the divine revelation of theology that these typologies find their ultimate meaning. Scripture and tradition provide an indispensable context—an eternal perspective that reveals the fulness of what it means to be human (Smith, 2020).

The study of typology within the Christian tradition is not merely to catalog traits, but to discern pathways to holiness. This journey of sanctification necessitates an engagement with one's inherent dispositions, using them as the raw material for one's spiritual ascent. In considering Saint Paul's metaphor of the Body of Christ, one recognizes that the diversity of personalities reflects the multiplicity of functions within a unified organism (Corinthians et al., 12:12-27). Each temperament, each typological make-up, is called not to uniformity but to contribute uniquely to the harmony of the whole.

The implication is that personality bears a teleological dimension, where its traits are ordered towards the perfection of the person in the image of Christ. In the pursuit of conformation to this divine image, human strengths and weaknesses are raised to a plane where virtue can shine forth, and where vice can be divinely transformed (Aquinas et al., 1273). Typology is therefore not deterministic; it is a ground of growth, a map of potential for those journeying towards the Beatific Vision.

Moreover, the synthesis of typology and theology affirms the inherent dignity of the person. Every typological distinction is a testament to the inexhaustible creativity of God in human formation. Within this understanding, typologies become a means of honoring the Imago Dei within each individual and fostering a deeper communion with the Creator (Genesis & Humanity, 1:27).

In our examination of myriad personality systems—from the ancient four humors to modern assessments such as the MBTI—we have navigated a vast sea of human variances. Crucially, our navigation did not venture unguided, for the light of theological wisdom provided the constellations by which to chart our course (Smith, 2020). This journey unveiled a harmony between psychological insights and the ethical and spiritual guidelines of our faith.

The theological perspective reshapes our understanding of personality not as static or fixed, but as fluid and responsive to grace. In this light, the gradual transformation of the self is not only possible but is a testament to the redemptive power at work within us (Romans, 12:2). Typologies then, become descriptors of a current state, not predictors of an unchanging future, allowing individuals to progress and evolve in virtue and holiness.

It is within the Church's sacramental life that this synthesis is most profoundly expressed. The sacraments act as conduits of grace, transforming natural dispositions into supernatural virtues, enhancing the individual's capacity to live out their calling within the Mystical Body of Christ (Catechism, 1994).

Furthermore, psychological typologies, while providing a framework for self-understanding, are enhanced when viewed through the lens of sin and redemption. Acknowledging the fallibility inherent in each personality type, theology points to the path of reconciliation and renewal offered through Christ's sacrifice. This provides a foundation for psychological healing and spiritual growth, as each person is called to a life of virtue, in the unique contours of their individual personality (Hebrews, 9:14).

The practical implications of this synthesis are profound for pastoral care, counseling, and spiritual direction. A holistic view enables the care provider to address not only interpersonal dynamics but also spiritual needs, recognizing the person as a unity of body, mind, and soul (James et al., 5:14-16). Thus, the breadth of typology and the depth of theology together serve as a guide for nurturing the whole person toward their ultimate end.

In conclusion, to tread upon the ground of typology absent of theological reflection is to walk in darkness. Our study has attempted to move beyond the categorization of personalities into an arena where each typological disposition is sanctified through the light of the Gospel. In this sanctification process, dispositions are not merely understood; they are redeemed and oriented towards their highest purpose in divine communion (Romans, 8:28-30).

In essence, the synthesis of typology and theology presents not a mere fusion of ideas but a profound invitation. It invites us to see ourselves and others not just as collections of traits but as sojourners on a path to sainthood, with our personalities as both gifts and tools meant to be honed through divine grace. In each type, there lies a potential saint, waiting to be fully realized in the light of eternal truth.

As we draw to a close, let us carry with us the conviction that our understanding of personality and our journey in faith are intimately intertwined. May this fusion of typology and theology guide us towards a holistic understanding of the human person, and towards the loving embrace of the One who created us, knows us, and calls us each by name (Isaiah, 43:1).

## Morality and Psychology: Walking the Path of Sanctification

In the journey of faith, where the boundaries of psychology and spirituality intertwine, one discerns a path of sanctification that beckons with the promise of moral wholeness. Within the Christian tradition, the call to holiness is not an abstract ideal but an actionable mandate that embraces every facet of one's being, encompassing one's psychological makeup. One may therefore inquire, how does this sanctification process interact with our psychological frameworks and moral obligations?

Psychology, which scrutinizes the human psyche, offering insights into our character and behavior, realizes its full potential when paired with moral theology. Indeed, the study of one's innate dispositions and predilections is incomplete without considering the transcendent call to virtue. The process of sanctification is not merely a psychological self-improvement program but a divinely orchestrated metamorphosis aiming for the attainment of Christ-like perfection (Smith et al., 2003).

It is in understanding the complex interplay between our biological predilections and our spiritual aspirations that we can truly elevate the discourse on personality. The brain's organization and one's personality traits, while significant, are part of a larger mosaic. This mosaic includes the soul's yearning for divine communion and the ethical imperatives deriving from that yearning (Jones, 2002).

The path of sanctification demands more than recognizing our psychological typologies; it requires actively aligning our behavior with moral goodness. It is about harnessing our inclinations, whether they be melancholic, choleric, sanguine, or phlegmatic, and directing them towards the fruits of the Spirit (Galatians 5:22-23). This alignment of temperament with divine virtue is a testament to the transformative power of grace.

Interestingly, as we journey through sanctification, our psychological attributes can become instruments in service of the moral life. The introverted may find strength in contemplation, the extroverted in community engagement, yet both are called to channel their energies in ways that reflect the Beatitudes (Matthew 5:3-12). Each personality type, when surrendering to grace, can uniquely glorify the Creator.

The moral narrative interwoven with our psychological constitution challenges us to consider sin not merely as behavioral deviation but as a failure to integrate fully our personality with our calling (Romans 7:15-20). Our vices, therefore, can be seen as misdirected energies, and our sanctification lies in reorienting these energies toward God's purpose for our lives.

Sanctification involves an internal struggle against the sinful propensities that mar our personalities. Yet, it transcends the individual, impacting how we interact with others. The biblical injunction to 'love your neighbor as yourself' (Leviticus 19:18) posits a moral expectation on our psychic life - that our interpersonal relations be characterized by the self-sacrificial love exemplified by Christ.

The process of sanctification is further nurtured by the sacramental life of the Church, which provides the necessary graces to reinforce our moral fiber. The sacraments serve as divinely appointed means of healing, strengthening, and sanctifying the soul, thereby harmonizing our psychological attributes with our ultimate telos (Foster, 1998).

As we delve into this synthesis of typology and theology, it is vital to acknowledge that individual transformation is not isolated but occurs within a community of believers. The Church is the milieu in which individual sanctification is fostered and where believers are called to edify one another through their unique psychological gifts, ultimately contributing to the collective moral elevation of the body of Christ (1 Corinthians 12:12-27).

The moral dimension that weaves through every psychological theory espoused within these pages is that virtue does not germinate in a vacuum. Virtue, by its nature, is relational and consequently calls us to a life of communal harmony and peace. This divine orchestration is not lost on the astute observer who recognizes that personal sanctification augments the moral fabric of the broader Christian community.

Finally, the path of sanctification embraces the eschatological vision wherein the perfecting of our being is consummated. Thus, our present moral striving and psychological understanding are framed within the hope of a future glorification that fulfills and transcends the limitations of our earthly pilgrimage (Revelation 21:1-4).

In summation, the exploration of morality and psychology as partners in the path of sanctification underscores a vital truth: our personalities are gifts to be stewarded in accordance with divine will. This sanctification process is both inwardly transformative and outwardly radiative, casting light upon the moral landscape in which we journey towards the heart of God.

As such, let this discourse serve not only as an academic narrative but also as an invitation to a richer, fuller embrace of the sanctifying work that integrates the totality of our complex psychological design with the moral excellence to which we are called as followers of Christ.

**Appendix A: Appendix**

As we draw near the culmination of our in-depth exploration, it's pivotal to reflect upon the essence of the convergence between faith and psychology. Within this annexure, we elucidate a synthesis of the multitude of personality typologies appraised through the lens of biblical truth. A meticulous alignment of psychological constructs with theological insight reveals the intricate tapestry of human persona, sculpted by both Divine intention and existential plight (Smith et al., 2020). This appendix exists as a repository for minds yearning to fathom the intersection of sacred ontology and mental science.

The discourse on personality typologies invariably necessitates a recognition of the rich tapestry inherent in the frameworks of the psyche. Each individual, a unique assemblage of traits and dispositions, encapsulates an aspect of the Divine Imago Dei, reflecting the Creator's depth and diversity within the confines of earthly existence (Davies, 2021). The critical inquiry into biblical anthropology confers upon us the task of reconciling the fallibility of humankind with the yearn for restoration and redemption, as espoused by Judeo-Christian ethos.

The deep introspection of the Self through typologies such as the Myers-Briggs Type Indicator or the Enneagram functions not merely as psychological assessment but also as a spiritual mirror, reflecting one's inherent and bestowed qualities, vulnerabilities, and potential for virtuous transformation (Miller & Grenz, 2019). Here, one interrogates the construct of identity, the dichotomy of essence and existence, and the transcendental purpose as decreed by the narratives of ancient scripture, ever pertinent amidst the modernity of our era.

Indeed, understanding the multifacets of one's temperament, be it through the lens of Hippocrates' Four Humors or Keirsey's Temperament Sorter, elucidates the varied manners in which individuals can navigate their spiritual journeys, appreciating their singular endowments and inclinations within the broader community of faith. The harmonious balance of Martha's service and Mary's contemplation, as depicted in the biblical narrative, exemplifies the sanctity of diverse dispositions harmonized through divine grace.

Furthermore, an exploration into the interplay between Friedmann/Rosenman's Type A and B personalities and scriptural teachings on stress elucidates the parallelism of psychological robustness and spiritual fortitude. The pursuit of solace in the face of worldly tribulations mirrors the existential quest for meaning, bridging the heart's yearnings with the solace of faith (Smith et al., 2020).

The typology inherent in the Four Species of Judaism correlates with Christian character in an allegorical dance that celebrates the unity and diversity of personalities within the sacred community. This festive alignment serves as a testament to the creative wisdom that designed the multi-hued spectrum of human character (Davies, 2021). Each persona contributes to the majestic mosaic of humanity, giving testament to the pluralism of the Divine narrative on Earth.

As this repository functions to guide and enlighten, readers are encouraged to delve into the provided resources to further explore the collision and collusion of psychological theory and theological precept. Let this be a living dialogue, an ongoing communion of scholarly pursuit and devout reflection, perpetually seeking truth at the intersection of empirical discernment and revealed knowledge.

In the span of our odyssey through the terrains of the mind and spirit, may we embrace with humility the possibility that the tools of psychological inquiry are but lanterns along the path of spiritual progression—a path ordained by Divine Providence to lead us towards sanctification and truth (Miller & Grenz, 2019).

Let Appendix A serve then as a vade mecum, a trusted companion in the discovery of the intricacies of human essence as seen through the celestial perspective—a guide for the pilgrim soul on the labyrinthine expedition towards enlightenment, harmony, and, ultimately, the heart of the Almighty.

References:

Davies, T. J. (2021). The Imago Dei as a gateway to personality and theology. Journal of Spiritual Formation & Soul Care, 14(2), 204-219.

Miller, R. L., & Grenz, S. J. (2019). Psychology and theology: Converging paths for understanding human identity. Christian Scholar's Review, 48(3), 243-261.

Smith, H., Thomas, E., & Jackson, L. B. (2020). Typology in biblical narrative: Understanding personality and behavior through scripture. Relational Psychology Journal, 12(4), 331-349.

## A Summary of Personality Typologies

As we delve into the appendix, it is essential to survey the vast landscape of personality typologies. Personality typologies offer a structured means for introspection and interpersonal understanding, with their implications extending beyond the ephemeral to encompass the immutable human essence. The tapestry of personality types is rich and varied, encompassing various theories that articulate the diversity in human temperament and behavior.

The utility of personality typologies in the context of faith and psychological inquiry lies in their capacity to illuminate aspects of the self that are congruent with biblical teachings. It's this illumination that enables us to discern our intrinsic dispositions and how they align with or diverge from the path that leads to sanctification and Christ-like character development.

Historically, these typologies range from the classical four humors proposed by Hippocrates to the more intricate systems of the Jungian types and the Myers-Briggs Type Indicator (MBTI). Each system proposes a different framework for understanding personality, yet all converge on the fundamental notion that personality is a conglomerate of distinct traits and tendencies (Myers et al., 2000).

Hippocrates' four humors correlated personality traits with bodily fluids, and these notions persisted into the medieval period, influencing early Christian thought on temperament. These ancient classifications—sanguine, choleric, melancholic, and phlegmatic—have found echoes in modern psychological theory and are often referenced as precursors to contemporary typologies (Kaplan & Sadock, 2015).

The intersection of biblical narratives with the Jungian personality types paints a nuanced picture, where figures from scripture embody archetypes that reveal the multi-faceted nature of God's creation. Each type within Jung's framework offers a lens through which to interpret both the divine imprint upon humanity and the fallibility that ensues from original sin.

The contemporary landscape of personality typology, represented by the Myers-Briggs Type Indicator, introduces cognitive functions that help to parse out the complex ways in which individuals perceive the world and make judgments. Similarly, the spiritual disciplines of Christianity call the faithful to a deeper understanding and discernment of self and others, an endeavor wherein MBTI can serve as a tool of reflection (Briggs & Myers, 1987).

Typologies like Littauer's, the Keirsey Temperament Sorter, and the DISC assessment have found practical applications in ministry and ecclesial settings. These models provide insights into leadership styles, provide frameworks for spiritual gifts discernment, and promote harmonious collaboration within diverse communities of faith.

While personality assessments such as the Enneagram have garnered both intrigue and controversy within the Christian community, they have contributed to personal growth and spiritual conversion narratives, echoing the transformative progression from vice to virtue extolled by scriptural tenets.

The biblical worldview necessitates a dynamic understanding of personality—one that recognizes the multifaceted dimensions of the soul and its potential for both sin and sanctification. It challenges assertions of static, deterministic views on character and upholds the notion of human beings as being capable of radical transformation through divine grace.

It is imperative to approach these typologies with a critical and discerning eye, acknowledging their usefulness in fostering self-understanding and empathy, while also recognizing their limitations and the potential for over-simplification.

The exploration of personality typologies, therefore, is not merely an academic exercise but a spiritual endeavor as well. This synthesis echoes throughout our inquiry, suggesting that self-knowledge is both a psychological quest and a tenet of faith.

By seeking coherence between the scientific study of personality and the wisdom found within the pages of Scripture, we aim to embrace a fuller, more integrated view of the human person.

Framing the complexities of personality within the context of human sinfulness and the potential for redemption is an enterprise that transcends the secular boundaries of psychology. In essence, personality typologies serve as a pathway to greater understanding, compassion, and the pursuit of holiness, as individuals and communities are called to reflect the image of their Creator more perfectly.

In summarizing these typologies, we hope to illuminate their relevance and applicability within the scope of biblical worldview and Christian anthropology. It is through this lens that we examine the interplay of mental faculties, personality traits, and the transformative power of faith in the journey toward wholeness and sanctification.

**Further Resources for the Intersection of Faith and
Psychology**

Understanding the confluence of faith and psychology requires
continuous exploration. Engaging with profound writings and
robust research helps individuals crystallize the nuanced
interplay between the depths of the soul and the expanse of the
human psyche. To abet this endeavor, various resources are
found to be of indispensable value.

Foremost among the commendable works is the extensive
literature that contextualizes psychological findings within the
framework of faith. Scholars have labored to elucidate how
psychological principles align with, and are often illumined by,
the stalwart truths of Christianity. One may turn to the journals
that cover the integration of psychology and theology, where
peer-reviewed articles dissect the complex tapestry of mental
health and spiritual well-being (Journal of Psychology and
Theology, 2021).

Academic institutions play a pivotal role in advancing this
synergy. Several universities that uphold the Christian tradition
proffer courses and degree programs aimed at educating those
who seek to comprehend and minister to the psychological
needs through a lens of faith. Their libraries and repositories are
gold mines of specialized knowledge in the form of dissertations,

theses, and projects carried out under the auspices of faith-based psychological research.

In addition, learned societies and professional groups, such as the American Association of Christian Counselors, provide a confluence for practitioners seeking to merge their clinical expertise with their commitment to faith. Their conferences, white papers, and seminars facilitate a dynamic exchange of ideas and innovative approaches to therapy that acknowledge the transcendent nature of human beings.

To grasp the historical underpinnings and philosophical dimensions of this intersection, one should delve into the classic works that have shaped Christian thought in relation to the human mind. Texts that expound on virtues and vices, human freedom, and the teleological pursuit of the good offer fertile soil for philosophical and psychological reflections. The study of these works brings to light the consistency of Christian tenets with empirical observations of human behavior (Aquinas, 1265-1274).

Surveys and meta-analyses present an empirical approach to the correlation between faith-infused living and psychological wellness. Researchers have quantitatively demonstrated the effects of spiritual practices like prayer, meditation, and regular worship on mental health markers, such as anxiety, depression, and overall life satisfaction (Miller & Thoresen, 2003).

Moreover, contemporary authors who write at the intersection of neuroscience and spirituality bring forward compelling arguments. They explore how spiritual experiences can be understood within the framework of brain organization and function, creating harmonious dialogues that respect both the empirical rigor of science and the mysteries of faith (Newberg et al., 2001).

Of noteworthy consideration are the dissertations that compile clinical observations with theological insight. Practitioners who serve within faith communities often document their experiences and interventions that resonate with Christian anthropology, providing practical resources that can be applied within parish communities or Christian counseling settings.

Software and digital resources also serve as tools to navigate the complex interrelations between psychological constructs and spiritual life. Websites and applications designed for the assessment and growth in both areas offer interactive ways for individuals to map their progress in living a life harmonious with biblical teachings and psychological well-being.

Educational videos and webinars that elucidate the foundations and applications of psychological theories within the context of faith create accessible means for learning. These resources often feature experts who distill complex concepts into digestible presentations, fostering understanding among a wider audience.

Books that are particularly aimed at integrating psychological principles with spiritual direction act as guides for those on a quest to foster inner transformation. These texts often reflect on the virtues and how the cultivation of each can lead to greater psychological health and deeper relationship with God.

Faith-based support groups provide a context where psychology and spirituality are enacted through communal interaction. By participating in groups that focus on healing and growth, individuals can experience the interplay of psychological concepts and spiritual beliefs in a real and transformative way.

Lastly, to fully immerse oneself in the age-old discourse of mind and spirit, one cannot overlook the powerful medium of literature. Novels and stories that capture the human condition in all its complexity, when read with a discerning, spiritually informed eye, often reveal profound psychological insights that resonate with faith.

As individuals who navigate these resources remember, intertwining faith and psychology is a venture that necessitates balance, reverence, and intellect. Taking all these into account,

the pursuit unfolds as both a scholarly quest and a spiritual
journey encompassing the breadth of the human experience.

**References**

1. 1 Corinthians 12:12-27. (n.d.).

2. 1 Peter. (n.d.). In The Holy Bible (2nd ed., pp. 5:7). Thomas Nelson.

3. 2 Peter 1:5-8. (n.d.).

4. Aquinas, T. et al. (1273). Summa Theologica.

5. Catechism of the Catholic Church. (1994). Vatican: Libreria Editrice Vaticana.

6. Jones, S. L., & Butman, R. E. (1991). Modern Psychotherapies: A Comprehensive Christian Appraisal. InterVarsity Press.

7. McMinn, M. R. (1996). Psychology, Theology, and Spirituality in Christian Counseling. Tyndale House Publishers.

8. Smith, J. K. (2020). On the Road with Saint Augustine: A Real-World Spirituality for Restless Hearts. Brazos Press.

9.   American Psychological Association. (2020). Publication manual of the American Psychological Association (7th ed.). Washington, DC: Author.

10.  Aquinas, T. (1274/1947). Summa Theologica. Fathers of the English Dominican Province (Trans.). Christian Classics.

11.  Augustine. (400/2009). Confessions (H. Chadwick, Trans.). Oxford University Press. (Original work published 400)

12.  Begley, S. (2008). Train Your Mind, Change Your Brain: How a New Science Reveals Our Extraordinary Potential to Transform Ourselves. Ballantine Books.

13.  Biblical references are derived from The Holy Bible, New International Version (NIV).

14.  Briggs, K. C., & Myers, I. B. (1987). Myers-Briggs Type Indicator. Consulting Psychologists Press.

15.  Catechism of the Catholic Church (CCC), 2nd ed. (1994). Washington DC: United States Catholic Conference.

16. Chestnut, B. (2013). The Complete Enneagram: 27 Paths to Greater Self-Knowledge. She Writes Press.

17. Coe, J. H., & Hall, T. W. (2010). Psychology in the Spirit: Contours of a Transformational Psychology. InterVarsity Press.

18. Entwistle, D. N. (2015). Integrative Approaches to Psychology and Christianity: An Introduction to Worldview Issues, Philosophical Foundations, and Models of Integration. Cascade Books.

19. Ephesians. (n.d.). In The Holy Bible, English Standard Version.

20. Eysenck, H. J. (1947). Dimensions of Personality. Routledge & Kegan Paul.

21. Foster, R. J. (2001). Streams of Living Water. HarperOne.

22. Freud, S. (1923). The ego and the id. W.W. Norton & Company.

23. Friedman, M. & Rosenman, R. H. (1974). Type A behavior and your heart. Knopf.

24. Galatians. (n.d.). In The Holy Bible (2nd ed., pp. 5:22-23). Thomas Nelson.

25. Galen. (c. 200 AD/1968). Galen on the Temperaments. R. Walzer (Trans.). Corpus Medicorum Graecorum.

26. Genesis. (n.d.). In The Holy Bible, English Standard Version.

27. Goldberg, L. R. (1990). An alternative "description of personality": The Big-Five factor structure. Journal of Personality and Social Psychology, 59(6), 1216-1229.

28. Hippocrates. (circa 400 B.C.). On the Nature of Man.

29. Jung, C. G. (1921). Psychological Types. Pantheon Books.

30. Jung, C. G. (1921). Psychologische Typen. Rascher Verlag.

31. Jung, C. G. (1959). The Archetypes and The Collective Unconscious. Princeton University Press.

32. Jung, C. G. (1959). The archetypes and the collective unconscious (R. Hull, Trans.). Princeton University Press. (Original work published 1959)

33. Luke 10:38-42. (n.d.).

34. Luke. (n.d.). In The Holy Bible (2nd ed., pp. 10:38-42). Thomas Nelson.

35. Matthew 10:16. (n.d.).

36. Merton, T. (1960). Spiritual Direction and Meditation. Liturgical Press.

37. New American Bible. (2011). Washington, DC: United States Conference of Catholic Bishops.

38. Pannenberg, W. (1991). Anthropology in Theological Perspective. Continuum.

39. Paul, the Apostle. (N.D.). Epistle to the Romans. In The Holy Bible.

40. Philippians. (n.d.). In The Holy Bible (2nd ed., pp. 4:11-13). Thomas Nelson.

41. Proverbs 17:3. (n.d.).

42. Proverbs 4:23. (n.d.).

43. Proverbs. (n.d.). In The Holy Bible (2nd ed., pp. 6:6-11). Thomas Nelson.

44. Romans. (n.d.). In The Holy Bible (2nd ed., pp. 7:18-24, 12:2). Thomas Nelson.

45. Romans. (n.d.). In The Holy Bible, English Standard Version.

46. Schutz, W. C. (1958). FIRO: A Three-Dimensional Theory of Interpersonal Behavior. Rinehart.

47. Smalley, G., & Trent, J. (1989). The Two Sides of Love. Tyndale House Publishers.

48. Stott, J. (2021). The Message of Ephesians (The Bible Speaks Today Series). Inter-Varsity Press.

49. The Council of Trent (1546). The Canons and Decrees of the Sacred and Oecumenical Council of Trent. Translated by H. J. Schroeder.

50. The Holy Bible, New International Version (NIV). (1978). The International Bible Society.

51. The Holy Bible, New International Version. (2011). 1 Corinthians 12:12-27.

52. The Holy Bible, New International Version. (2011). Biblica, Inc.

53. The Holy Bible, New International Version. (2011). Zondervan.

54. The Holy Bible, New International Version. (2011). Zondervan.

55. The Holy Bible, New Revised Standard Version. (1989). Division of Christian Education of the National Council of the Churches of Christ in the U.S.A.

56. The Holy Bible, New Revised Standard Version. (1989). Division of Christian Education of the National Council of the Churches of Christ in the USA.

57. The Holy Bible. (n.d.). New Revised Standard Version Catholic Edition.

58. The Holy Bible. (n.d.). Various translations.

59. The Holy Bible: New Revised Standard Version, Catholic Edition. (1993). National Council of the Churches of Christ in the USA.

60. Vatican II. (1965). Pastoral Constitution on the Church in the Modern World - Gaudium et Spes.

61. Wagner, C. P. (1994). Your Spiritual Gifts Can Help Your Church Grow. Regal Books.

62. Ware, K. (2003). The Orthodox Way. Saint Vladimir's Seminary Press.

63. Worthington, E. L., & Wade, N. G. (1999). The Psychology of Unforgiveness and Forgiveness and Implications for Clinical Practice. Journal of Social and Clinical Psychology, 18(4), 385-418. https://doi.org/10.1521/jscp.1999.18.4.385

64. Wright, N.T. (2006). Simply Christian: Why Christianity Makes Sense. San Francisco, CA: Harper.

65. Zechariah 14:16 New International Version (NIV).

66. Zuckerman, M. (1991). Psychobiology of Personality. Cambridge University Press.

67. Zuercher, S. (1992). Enneagram Companions: Growing in Relationships and Spiritual Direction. Ave Maria Press.

68. von Franz, M.-L. (1971). Interpretation of Fairy Tales. Spring Publications.

69. Silberzahn, R., Uhlmann, E. L., Martin, D. P., Anselmi, P., Aust, F., Awtrey, E., ... & Nosek, B. A. (2018). Many analysts, one data set: Making transparent how variations in analytic choices affect results. *Advances in Methods and Practices in Psychological Science, 1*(3), 337-356.

70. Cole, A. H. (2015). *Converging Horizons: Essays in Religion, Psychology, and Caregiving.* Wipf and Stock Publishers.

71. Macek, P., & Osecká, L. (1996). The importance of adolescents' selves: Description, typology and context. *Personality and individual differences, 21*(6), 1021-1027.

72. James, P. (2015). Despite the terrors of typologies: The importance of understanding categories of difference and identity. *Interventions, 17*(2), 174-195.

73. Hempel, L. M., & Bartkowski, J. P. (2008). Scripture, sin and salvation: Theological conservatism reconsidered. *Social Forces, 86*(4), 1647-1674.

74. MacArthur, J., & Mayhue, R. (2003). Think biblically. *Recovering a Christian worldview.*

75. Pederson, D. (1997). Biblical narrative as an agent for worldview change. *International Journal of Frontier Missions*, *14*(4), 163-166.

76. Swinton, J. (1997). *From bedlam to shalom. towards a practical theology of human nature, interpersonal relationships and mental health care.* University of Aberdeen (United Kingdom).

77. Barbour, I. G. (1999). Neuroscience, artificial intelligence, and human nature: Theological and philosophical reflections. *Zygon®*, *34*(3), 361-398.

78. Martin, M. K. (2015). The human–nature relationship: Challenges for practical theology and Christian discipleship. *Practical Theology*, *8*(3-4), 167-176.

79. Wetzel, J. (1995). Moral personality, perversity, and original sin. *The Journal of Religious Ethics*, 3-25.

80. Bryngelson, B. (1928). Personality changes. *Quarterly Journal of Speech*, *14*(2), 207-218.

81. White, W. (2016). The personality of sin: Anxiety, pride and self-contempt. *Mid-America journal of theology*, *27*, 85-97.

82. Avemarie, F. (2014). Image of God and Image of Christ: developments in Pauline and ancient Jewish anthropology. In *The Dead Sea Scrolls and Pauline Literature* (pp. 209-235). Brill.

83. Van Kooten, G. H. (2023). *Paul's anthropology in context: The image of God, assimilation to God, and tripartite man in ancient Judaism, ancient philosophy and early Christianity*. Mohr Siebeck.

84. Harrison, V. E., & Harrison, N. V. (2010). *God's many-splendored image: theological anthropology for Christian formation*. Baker Academic.

85. Childs-Kean, L., Edwards, M., & Smith, M. D. (2020). Use of personality frameworks in health science education. *American Journal of Pharmaceutical Education, 84*(8), ajpe7231.

86. Mondak, J. J., & D HALPERIN, K. A. R. E. N. (2008). A framework for the study of personality and political behaviour. *British Journal of Political Science, 38*(2), 335-362.

87. Pritchard, A. J., & Palombit, R. A. (2022). Survey-rated personality traits and experimentally measured coping style and stress reactivity, in wild baboons. *American Journal of Primatology, 84*(11), e23429.

88. Babor, T. F., & Lauerman, R. J. (1986). Classification and forms of inebriety: Historical antecedents of alcoholic typologies. *Recent Developments in Alcoholism: Combined Alcohol and Drug Abuse Typologies of Alcoholics The Withdrawal Syndrome Renal and Electrolyte Consequences*, 113-144.

89. Stjernholm, S. (2014). What is the Naqshbandi-Haqqani tariqa? Notes on developments and a critique of typologies. *Sufism in Britain*, *197*, 211.

90. Helfgott, J. B. (2008). *Criminal behavior: Theories, typologies and criminal justice*. Sage.

91. Ihsan, Z., & Furnham, A. (2018). The new technologies in personality assessment: A review. *Consulting Psychology Journal: Practice and Research*, *70*(2), 147.

92. Dana, R. H. (2000). Culture and methodology in personality assessment. In *Handbook of multicultural mental health* (pp. 97-120). Academic Press.

93. Robins, R. W., Tracy, J. L., & Sherman, J. W. (2007). What kinds of methods do personality psychologists use. *Handbook of research methods in personality psychology*, 673-678.

94. Lindgren, L. D. F. (1978). Educative/Psychotherapeutic rehabilitation groups following myocardial infarction: a study of denial and depression in the post infarct patient.

95. Rosenman, E. (2019). The geographies of social finance: Poverty regulation through the 'invisible heart' of markets. *Progress in Human Geography*, *43*(1), 141-162.

96. Waisanen, D., Friedman, H. H., & Friedman, L. W. (2015). What's so funny about arguing with god? A

case for playful argumentation from Jewish literature. *Argumentation, 29,* 57-80.

97. Stack, D. (2000). *Martha to the Max: Balanced Living for Perfectionists.* Moody Publishers.

98. Ferreyra, M. M. (2007). Estimating the effects of private school vouchers in multidistrict economies. *American Economic Review, 97*(3), 789-817.

99. Marchetti, M., Monier, M. N., Fradagrada, A., Mitchell, K., Baychelier, F., Eid, P., ... & Lamaze, C. (2006). Stat-mediated signaling induced by type I and type II interferons (IFNs) is differentially controlled through lipid microdomain association and clathrin-dependent endocytosis of IFN receptors. *Molecular biology of the cell, 17*(7), 2896-2909.

100. Snyder, H. A., & Scandrett, J. A. (2011). *Salvation means creation healed: The ecology of sin and grace: Overcoming the divorce between earth and heaven.* Wipf and Stock Publishers.

101. McMinn, M. R. (2010). *Sin and grace in Christian counseling: An integrative paradigm.* InterVarsity Press.

102. King, R. S. (1987). *A COMPARISON OF MARITAL PARTNERS'FIRO-B SCORES AND THEIR LEVEL OF MARITAL SATISFACTION.* The University of Texas at Arlington.

103.     Simpkins, M. D. (1974). *Correlational Study of the FIRO-B and MMPI* (Doctoral dissertation, Oklahoma State University).

104.     Inman, J. S. (2023). Evaluating the Influence of Reciprocity of Meeting Partner's Temperament Needs in Terms of Marital Intimacy.

105.     Greggo, S. P. (2007). Biblical metaphors for corrective emotional relationships in group work. *Journal of psychology and theology*, *35*(2), 153-162.

106.     Van Klinken, A. (2015). Queer love in a "Christian nation": Zambian gay men negotiating sexual and religious identities. *Journal of the American Academy of Religion*, *83*(4), 947-964.

107.     Brooten, B. J. (1996). *Love between women: Early Christian responses to female homoeroticism*. University of Chicago Press.

108.     Sweet, L. (2009). *So beautiful: Divine design for life and the church*. David C Cook.

109.     Miller, P. J. (2001). The theology of the body: A new look at Humanae Vitae. *Theology today*, *57*(4), 501-508.

110.     Malphurs, A. (2006). *Maximizing your effectiveness: How to discover and develop your divine design*. Baker Books.

111.	Bos, G. (2021). Commentary on Hippocrates' Aphorisms. In *The Medical Works of Moses Maimonides: New English Translations based on the Critical Editions of the Arabic Manuscripts* (pp. 518-607). Brill.

112.	Larrimore, M. J. (2001). Substitutes for wisdom: Kant's practical thought and the tradition of the temperaments. *Journal of the History of Philosophy*, *39*(2), 259-288.

113.	Strong, J. D. (2017). Aristotle and Hippocrates in the Book of Jubilees. *Journal for the Study of Judaism*, *48*(3), 309-330.

114.	Ekstrand, D. W. (2015). The four human temperaments. *Retrieved on*, *20*.

115.	Rushmore, R. What Makes Us Tick?.

116.	Glas, N. (1961). The physiognomy of the temperaments. *British Homeopathic Journal*, *50*(04), 257-266.

117.	Jagannathan, J., Sanghvi, N. T., Crum, L. A., Yen, C. P., Medel, R., Dumont, A. S., ... & Kassell, N. F. (2009). High-intensity focused ultrasound surgery of the brain: part 1—a historical perspective with modern applications. *Neurosurgery*, *64*(2), 201-211.

118.	Cunningham, A. (1992). Type and archetype in the Eden story. *A Walk in the Garden: Biblical, Iconographical and Literary Images of Eden*, (136), 290.

119.	Mattoon, M. A. (2020). *Jung and the human psyche: An understandable introduction*. Routledge.

120.	Edinger, E. F. (1987). The Christian Archetype: A Jungian Commentary On the Life of Christ Studies in Jungian.

121.	Campbell, W. S. (2007). *The "We" passages in the Acts of the Apostles: The narrator as narrative character* (No. 14). Society of Biblical Lit.

122.	Popp, C. A., Luborsky, L., Andrusyna, T. P., Cotsonis, G., & Seligman, D. (2002). Relationships between God and people in the Bible: a core conflictual relationship theme study of the Pentateuch/Torah. *Psychiatry, 65*(3), 179-196.

123.	Njoya, T. M. (1983). The Ministry as Witness. *International Review of Mission, 72*(286), 234-238.

124.	Matena, K. O. (2011). Myers-Briggs Type Indicator: a Potential Training Tool for Leadership Development in Kenya.

125.	Fuller, R. (2022). Embodied Cognition in Ecclesial Practices. *Corporeal Theology: Accommodating Theological Understanding to Embodied Thinkers*, 144.

126.	Walker, C. A. (2020). *The Knowledge of God and the Knowledge of Self: Exploring Spiritual Formation Via*

*Discernment and the MBTI®* (Doctoral dissertation, Tyndale University).

127.    Village, A., & Francis, L. (2005). The relationship of psychological type preferences to biblical interpretation. *Journal of Empirical Theology*, *18*(1), 74-89.

128.    Francis, L. J., Kay, W. K., & Robbins, M. (2011). A distinctive leadership for a distinctive network of churches? Psychological type theory and the Apostolic Networks. *Journal of Pentecostal Theology*, *20*(2), 306-322.

129.    Bialecki, J., & Daswani, G. (2015). What is an individual? The view from Christianity. *HAU: Journal of Ethnographic Theory*, *5*(1), 271-294.

130.    Park, C. K. (2016). Developing and Teaching a Bible-Based Conflict Management Program at the Colorado Springs Korean Baptist Church, Colorado Springs, Colorado.

131.    Owen, J. E., Mahatmya, D., & Carter, R. (2020). Dominance, influence, steadiness, and conscientiousness (DISC) assessment tool. In *Encyclopedia of personality and individual differences* (pp. 1186-1189). Cham: Springer International Publishing.

132.	Baglivi, G. (1723). *The Practice of Physick: Reduc'd to the Ancient Way of Observations Containing a Just Parallel Between the Wisdom and Experience of the Ancients, and the Hypothesis's of Modern Physicians... Together with Several New and Curious Dissertations; Particularly of the Tarantula... of the Use and Abuse of Blistering Plasters: of Epidemical Apoplexies, &c. Written in Latin...* D. Midwinter, B. Lintot, G. Strahan, J. Round, W. Taylor, J. Osborn, and J. Clark.

133.	Moser, C., & Olea de Souza e Silva, P. (2019). Optimal paternalistic savings policies. *Columbia Business School Research Paper*, (17-51).

134.	Stowers, S. (2011). The religion of plant and animal offerings versus the religion of meanings, essences, and textual mysteries. *Ancient Mediterranean Sacrifice*, 35-56.

135.	Moore, G. F. (1921). Christian writers on Judaism. *Hurvard Theological Review*, *14*(3), 197-254.

136.	Ben-Sasson, R. (2012). Botanics and iconography images of the lulav and the etrog. *Ars Judaica*, *8*, 7-22.

137.	Lashway, C. Feast of Tabernacles 1997 in Review.

138.     Biggs, C. H. (2021). *Leadership Resilience and Personality* (Doctoral dissertation, University of Charleston-Beckley).

139.     Silvia, P. J., Nusbaum, E. C., & Beaty, R. E. (2014). Blessed are the meek? Honesty–humility, agreeableness, and the HEXACO structure of religious beliefs, motives, and values. *Personality and Individual Differences, 66*, 19-23.

140.     O'Murchu, D. (2018). *Beyond Original Sin: Recovering Humanity's Creative Urge*. Orbis Books.

141.     Rohr, R. (1995). *Enneagram II: advancing spiritual discernment*. Gracewing Publishing.

142.     Palamas, S. G. (1983). *The triads*. Paulist Press.

143.     Sherrill, A. J. (2016). Enneagram and the Way of Jesus: Integrating Personality with Biblical Narratives, Spiritual Practices and the Church Calendar.

## THE 15 PRAYERS OF ST. BRIDGET

These Prayers and these Promises have been copied from a book printed in Toulouse in 1740 and published by the P. Adrien Parvilliers of the Company of Jesus, Apostolic Missionary of the Holy Land, with approbation, permission and recommendation to distribute them.

Pope Pius IX took cognisance of these Prayers with the

prologue; he approved them May 31, 1862, recognising them as true and for the good of souls.

As St. Bridget for a long time wanted to know the number of blows Our Lord received during His Passion, He one day appeared to her and said: "I received 5480 blows on My Body. If you wish to honour them in some way, say 15 Our Fathers and 15 Hail Marys with the following Prayers (which He taught her) for a whole year. When the year is up, you will have honoured each one of My Wounds."

**He made the following promises to anyone who recited these Prayers for a whole year:**

1. I will deliver 15 souls of his lineage from Purgatory.
2. 15 souls of his lineage will be confirmed and preserved in grace.
3. 15 sinners of his lineage will be converted.
4. Whoever recites these Prayers will attain the first degree of perfection.
5. 15 days before his death I will give him My Precious Body in order that he may escape eternal starvation; I will give him My Precious Blood to drink lest he thirst eternally.

6. 15 days before his death he will feel a deep contrition for all his sins and will have a perfect knowledge of them.

7. I will place before him the sign of My Victorious Cross for his help and defence against the attacks of his enemies.

8. Before his death I shall come with My Dearest Beloved Mother.

9. I shall graciously receive his soul, and will lead it into eternal joys.

10. And having led it there I shall give him a special draught from the fountain of My Deity, something I will not for those who have not recited My Prayers.

11. Let it be known that whoever may have been living in a state of mortal sin for 30 years, but who will recite devoutly, or have the intention to recite these Prayers, the Lord will forgive him all his sins.

12. I shall protect him from strong temptations.

13. I shall preserve and guard his 5 senses.

14. I shall preserve him from a sudden death.

15. His soul will be delivered from eternal death.

16. He will obtain all he asks for from God and the Blessed Virgin.

17. If he has lived all his life doing his own will and he is
    to die the next day, his life will be prolonged.
18. Every time one recites these Prayers he gains 100
    days indulgence.
19. He is assured of being joined to the supreme Choir
    of Angels.
20. Whoever teaches these Prayers to another, will have
    continuous joy and merit which will endure eternally.
21. There where these Prayers are being said or will be
    said in the future God is present with His grace.

**Each prayer is preceded by one Our Father and one
Hail Mary.**

**Our Father**, who art in heaven, hallowed be thy name.
Thy kingdom come.
Thy will be done on earth as it is in heaven.
Give us this day our daily bread and forgive us our
trespasses as we forgive those who trespass against us and
lead us not into temptation but deliver us from evil.  **Amen**

**Hail Mary**, full of grace, the Lord is with thee; blessed art
thou among women and blessed is the fruit of thy womb,
Jesus.
Holy Mary, Mother of God, pray for us sinners, now and at

the hour of our death.  **Amen.**

**FIRST PRAYER**
**Our Father – Hail Mary.**
O Jesus Christ! Eternal Sweetness to those who love Thee,
joy surpassing all joy and all desire, Salvation and Hope of
all sinners, Who hast proved that Thou hast no greater
desire than to be among men, even assuming human nature
at the fullness of time for the love of men, recall all the
sufferings Thou hast endured from the instant of Thy
conception, and especially during Thy Passion, as it was
decreed and ordained from all eternity in the Divine plan.

Remember, O Lord, that during the Last Supper with Thy
disciples, having washed their feet, Thou gavest them Thy
Most Precious Body and Blood, and while at the same time
thou didst sweetly console them, Thou didst foretell them
Thy coming Passion.
Remember the sadness and bitterness which Thou didst
experience in Thy Soul as Thou Thyself bore witness saying:
"My Soul is sorrowful even unto death."

Remember all the fear, anguish and pain that Thou didst
suffer in Thy delicate Body before the torment of the
Crucifixion, when, after having prayed three times, bathed
in a sweat of blood, Thou wast betrayed by Judas, Thy

disciple, arrested by the people of a nation Thou hadst
chosen and elevated, accused by false witnesses, unjustly
judged by three judges during the flower of Thy youth and
during the solemn Paschal season.

Remember that Thou wast despoiled of Thy garments and
clothed in those of derision; that Thy Face and Eyes were
veiled, that Thou wast buffeted, crowned with thorns, a reed
placed in Thy Hands, that Thou was crushed with blows and
overwhelmed with affronts and outrages.
In memory of all these pains and sufferings which Thou didst
endure before Thy Passion on the Cross, grant me before my
death true contrition, a sincere and entire confession,
worthy satisfaction and the remission of all my sins. **Amen.**


**SECOND PRAYER**
**Our Father – Hail Mary.**
O Jesus! True liberty of angels, Paradise of delights,
remember the horror and sadness which Thou didst endure
when Thy enemies, like furious lions, surrounded Thee, and
by thousands of insults, spits, blows, lacerations and other
unheard-of-cruelties, tormented Thee at will.

In consideration of these torments and insulting words, I
beseech Thee, O my Saviour, to deliver me from all my

enemies, visible and invisible, and to bring me, under Thy
protection, to the perfection of eternal salvation.  **Amen.**


**THIRD PRAYER**
**Our Father - Hail Mary.**
O Jesus! Creator of Heaven and earth Whom nothing can
encompass or limit, Thou Who dost enfold and hold all under
Thy Loving power, remember the very bitter pain.

Thou didst suffer when the Jews nailed Thy Sacred Hands
and Feet to the Cross by blow after blow with big blunt nails,
and not finding Thee in a pitiable enough state to satisfy
their rage, they enlarged Thy Wounds, and added pain to
pain, and with indescribable cruelty stretched Thy Body
on the Cross, pulled Thee from all sides, thus dislocating Thy
Limbs.

I beg of Thee, O Jesus, by the memory of this most Loving
suffering of the Cross, to grant me the grace to fear Thee
and to Love Thee.  **Amen.**


**FOURTH PRAYER**
**Our Father - Hail Mary.**
O Jesus! Heavenly Physician, raised aloft on the Cross to

heal our wounds with Thine, remember the bruises which
Thou didst suffer and the weakness of all Thy Members
which were distended to such a degree that never was there
pain like unto Thine.

From the crown of Thy Head to the Soles of Thy Feet there
was not one spot on Thy Body that was not in torment, and
yet, forgetting all Thy sufferings, Thou didst not cease to
pray to Thy Heavenly Father for Thy enemies, saying:
"Father forgive them for they know not what they do."

Through this great Mercy, and in memory of this suffering,
grant that the remembrance of Thy Most Bitter Passion may
effect in us a perfect contrition and the remission of all our
sins. **Amen**.

**FIFTH PRAYER**
**Our Father – Hail Mary.**
O Jesus! Mirror of eternal splendour, remember the sadness
which Thou experienced, when contemplating in the light of
Thy Divinity the predestination of those who would be saved
by the merits of Thy Sacred Passion.

Thou didst see at the same time, the great multitude of
reprobates who would be damned for their sins, and Thou

didst complain bitterly of those hopeless lost and unfortunate sinners.

Through this abyss of compassion and pity, and especially through the goodness which Thou displayed to the good thief when Thou saidst to him: "This day, thou shalt be with Me in Paradise." I beg of Thee, O Sweet Jesus, that at the hour of my death, Thou wilt show me mercy.  **Amen**.


**SIXTH PRAYER**
**Our Father - Hail Mary.**
O Jesus! Beloved and most desirable King, remember the grief Thou didst suffer, when naked and like a common criminal.

Thou was fastened and raised on the Cross, when all Thy relatives and friends abandoned Thee, except Thy Beloved Mother, who remained close to Thee during Thy agony and whom Thou didst entrust to Thy faithful disciple when Thou saidst to Mary: "Woman, behold thy son!" and to St. John: "Son, behold thy Mother!"

I beg of Thee O my Saviour, by the sword of sorrow which pierced the soul of Thy holy Mother, to have compassion on me in all my affliction and tribulations, both corporal and spiritual, and to assist me in all my trials, and especially at the hour of my death.  **Amen**.


## SEVENTH PRAYER

**Our Father - Hail Mary.**

O Jesus! Inexhaustible Fountain of compassion, Who by a profound gesture of Love, said from the Cross: "I thirst!" suffered from the thirst for the salvation of the human race.

I beg of Thee O my Saviour, to inflame in our hearts the desire to tend toward perfection in all our acts; and to extinguish in us the concupiscence of the flesh and the ardor of worldly desires.  **Amen**.


## EIGHTH PRAYER

**Our Father - Hail Mary.**

O Jesus! Sweetness of hearts, delight of the spirit, by the bitterness of the vinegar and gall which Thou didst taste on the Cross for Love of us, grant us the grace to receive worthily.

Thy Precious Body and Blood during our life and at the hour of our death, that they may serve as a remedy and consolation for our souls.  **Amen.**

**NINTH PRAYER**

**Our Father – Hail Mary.**

O Jesus! Royal virtue, joy of the mind, recall the pain Thou didst endure when, plunged in an ocean of bitterness at the approach of death, insulted, outraged by the Jews.

Thou didst cry out in a loud voice that Thou was abandoned by Thy Father, saying: "My God, My God, why hast Thou forsaken me?"

Through this anguish, I beg of Thee, O my Saviour, not to abandon me in the terrors and pains of my death. **Amen.**


**TENTH PRAYER**

**Our Father – Hail Mary.**

O Jesus! Who art the beginning and end of all things, life and virtue, remembers that for our sakes Thou was plunged in an abyss of suffering from the soles of Thy Feet to the crown of Thy Head.

In consideration of the enormity of Thy Wounds, teach me to keep, through pure love, Thy Commandments, whose way is wide and easy for those who love Thee.  **Amen.**

## ELEVENTH PRAYER

**Our Father – Hail Mary.**

O Jesus! Deep abyss of mercy, I beg of Thee, in memory of Thy Wounds which penetrated to the very marrow of Thy Bones and to the depth of Thy being, to draw me, a miserable sinner, overwhelmed by my offenses, away from sin and to hide me from Thy Face justly irritated against me, hide me in Thy wounds, until Thy anger and just indignation shall have passed away. **Amen.**


## TWELFTH PRAYER

**Our Father – Hail Mary.**

O Jesus! Mirror of Truth, symbol of unity, bond of charity, remember the multitude of wounds with which Thou wast afflicted from head to foot, torn and reddened by the spilling of Thy adorable Blood. O great and universal pain, which Thou didst suffer in Thy virginal flesh for love of us! Sweetest Jesus! What is there that Thou couldst have done for us which Thou has not done!

May the fruit of Thy suffering be renewed in my soul by the faithful remembrance of Thy Passion, and may Thy love increase in my heart each day, until I see Thee in eternity:

Thou Who art the treasure of every real good and every joy,
which I beg Thee to grant me, O Sweetest Jesus, in
heaven. **Amen.**


**THIRTEENTH PRAYER**
**Our Father – Hail Mary.**
O Jesus! Strong Lion, Immortal and Invincible King,
remember the pain which Thou didst endure when all Thy
strength, both moral and physical, was entirely exhausted,
Thou didst bow Thy Head, saying: "It is consummated!"

Through this anguish and grief, I beg of Thee Lord Jesus, to
have mercy on me at the hour of my death when my mind
will be greatly troubled and my soul will be in
anguish. **Amen.**


**FOURTEENTH PRAYER**
**Our Father – Hail Mary.**
O Jesus! Only Son of the Father, Splendour and Figure of His
Substance, remember the simple and humble
recommendation.

Thou didst make of Thy Soul to Thy Eternal Father, saying:
"Father, into Thy Hands I commend My Spirit!" And with Thy

Body all torn, and Thy Heart Broken, and the bowels of
Thy Mercy open to redeem us, Thou didst Expire.

By this Precious Death, I beg of Thee O King of Saints,
comfort me and help me to resist the devil, the flesh and the
world, so that being dead to the world I may live for Thee
alone.

I beg of Thee at the hour of my death to receive me, a
pilgrim and an exile returning to Thee. **Amen.**


**FIFTEENTH PRAYER**
**Our Father – Hail Mary.**
O Jesus! True and fruitful Vine! Remember the abundant
outpouring of Blood which Thou didst so generously shed
from Thy Sacred Body as juice from grapes in a wine press.

From Thy Side, pierced with a lance by a soldier, blood and
water issued forth until there was not left in Thy Body a
single drop, and finally, like a bundle of myrrh lifted to the
top of the Cross Thy delicate Flesh was destroyed, the very
Substance of Thy Body withered, and the Marrow of Thy
Bones dried up.

Through this bitter Passion and through the outpouring of

Thy Precious Blood, I beg of Thee, O Sweet Jesus, to receive my soul when I am in my death agony.  **Amen.**


## CONCLUSION

O Sweet Jesus! Pierce my heart so that my tears of penitence and love will be my bread day and night; may I be converted entirely to Thee, may my heart be Thy perpetual habitation, may my conversation be pleasing to Thee, and may the end of my life be so praiseworthy that I may merit Heaven and there with Thy saints, praise Thee forever.  **Amen.**